JACKALS AT
JEKYLL

BY
RICHARD C. SIZEMORE

Bloomington, IN Milton Keynes, UK

authorHOUSE

AuthorHouse™
1663 Liberty Drive, Suite 200
Bloomington, IN 47403
www.authorhouse.com
Phone: 1-800-839-8640

AuthorHouse™ UK Ltd.
500 Avebury Boulevard
Central Milton Keynes, MK9 2BE
www.authorhouse.co.uk
Phone: 08001974150

First published by AuthorHouse   6/1/2006

ISBN: 1-4259-1244-3 (sc)

Printed in the United States of America
Bloomington, Indiana

This book is printed on acid-free paper.

Images courtesy of Jekyll Island Museum

CHAPTER I

November 22, 1910. Remember the date—a date of iniquity. That was the day the execution of the biggest scam in world history got underway, although the scheming had been going on for some time.

That was the start of negotiations for the secret plot that undid the work of the founding fathers who had framed the Constitution 123 years earlier. They had deliberately excluded the printing of fiat money not backed by gold or silver.

And that was the day that started the handover of the economy of the American people to a band of private bankers.

President Woodrow Wilson abetted the bankers with their plan and also gave a good dose of other socialist legislation including the income tax. The obscure New Jersey governor was promoted into office and used by the bankers. Other presidents and government operatives have aided the bankers' objectives since, but Wilson unwittingly abetted their original scheme and signed the legislation they wanted. Some historians and critics claim Wilson apparently did not understand that he was handing over a money monopoly to New York bankers.

The brazen scheme spawned in 1910 is still paying well for the offspring of those who pulled it off. Execution of the well-planned scheme began in a luxurious, private railway car in Hoboken, New Jersey, across the Hudson River from New York City.

The players, who hurried as separately and as secretly as they could to board the train, headed most of the nation's largest New York banks controlled by J. P. Morgan and Rockefeller oil money. A close associate of President William Howard Taft also was in the group. The ensemble was led by the most prestigious and intriguing member of the United States Senate and alleged front man for John D. Rockefeller. All the members of the band bore the facade of gentlemen and respectability. All, however, were nothing more than crooks engaged in a colossal conspiracy.

Yes, it was a CONSPIRACY, with a capital C, the word that makes the liberal Eastern press cringe and writers such as William Greider, former assistant managing editor of the *Washington Post*, rush to defend the elites against that accusation.

The scam was nothing less than a plot to gain control of the money and credit of the people of the United States and undermine the constitutional government on which the nation was founded. The plan was said to have been masterminded by Baron Alfred Rothschild of London and supported by big United States and international bankers. Technical details for executing the scheme were mostly left to a German immigrant who was not even an American citizen at the time.

Grieder, in his book *Secrets of the Temple* (p. 276), states, "The conspiracy-minded critics exaggerated the importance of the Jekyll Island meeting, since it was hardly a secret that Wall Street wanted (banking) reform." This in no way exonerates the bankers (then known as "the Bankers' Trust") from the charge of conspiracy, the definition of which is:

"An agreement between two or more persons to do an evil act in concert; A plot; Secret combinations of men for an evil purpose" (Funk and Wagnalls). The evil purpose was to get control of the money and credit of the United States and to form a banking monopoly. The secret meeting was a clear conspiracy or, as G. Edward Griffin stated in *The Creature from Jekyll Island*, "A classic example of a cartel structure."

All the apologies from the Eastern press won't wash out the true meaning of the conspiracy and cartel whose purpose was to set up a money monopoly that still exists today.

EVENTS OF THE DAY

It was an ordinary day in the nation's largest city. The weather, according to the *New York Times*, was cloudy with a rain forecast and a temperature range from thirty-five to forty-five degrees, accompanied by south to southwest winds. Some accounts say the weather grew cold with blustery winds by time to board the train.

Newspaper ads announced heavy orders were sending turkey prices up from twenty-five to twenty-eight to thirty cents a pound as Thanksgiving approached. The bankers had no concern about that. They were headed for even more extravagant menus than they were customarily used to when they reached their destination, a private resort off the southeast corner of Georgia—JEKYLL ISLAND.

The news on this early twentieth-century day was similar then to what we read in our newspapers almost a century later, according to the *New York Times*. It reported that a segregation ordinance had passed the city council in Baltimore, the latest information about the Mexican Revolution, several crime stories including a drive-by shooting, an item on the sports page that Yale University was getting a new stadium, and the obituary of Count Leo Tolstoy. There also was a two-paragraph story on the front page that financier J. P. Morgan was in Washington on what he called a social visit but which led to much speculation anyway. Apparently, even the *New York Times*, which was financed by Morgan money, wasn't putting his word in the bank.

The jackals perpetrating the grand scheme represented the world's money elite, and most were minions of Morgan, who himself represented the largest bankers of Europe, the Rothschilds, who had long been trying to get control of the Republic's money and credit.

Speculation on Morgan's Washington visit covered the Mexican War, a possible meeting with President William Howard Taft who was returning that day from a tour of Panama, or to be on hand for a hearing on railroad rates by the Interstate Commerce Commission. The possibility that Morgan might be trying to divert attention from the bankers' trip from New York south or to offer public proof he was not aboard the New York train never came up for speculation. Had the bankers been exposed, Morgan had an iron-clad alibi, although his geldings were present and plotting.

They were on their way to board the private railroad car of Senator Nelson Aldrich of Rhode Island that would be attached to the rear of a train headed southward. The setting would make any director of a cloak-and-dagger movie envious. The blinds of the private car were drawn tight, and only their amber outline was visible. Each individual had to make his way to the private car located on the New Jersey littoral of the Hudson as unobtrusively as possible.

First names were forbidden for fear of recognition. Two of the bankers referred to each other as Orville and Wilbur after the famous Wright brothers. Aldrich was called Zivil or Nelson. The scheming bankers and Washington politicians themselves were all prominent in their respective callings.

The plan had to be kept secret from the people who would have doomed it had they known about it. If caught, however, the bankers themselves would have been in no danger of prosecution, although their plot to set up a central bank and gain control of the nation's finances would have been foiled. The country was not too fond of New York bankers so soon after the panic of 1907, which some historians say they designed in their efforts to gain their objective. So, exposure must not happen.

The people who were to be fleeced must not understand the plan, and once it was molded into shape, it had to be disguised as something else by expensive propaganda before it could be presented for public scrutiny. This effort was to be led by paid professors of prestigious universities (Chicago, Harvard, and Princeton) so that Congress and the public would buy the proposed legislation.

SECRECY

The trip and the secrecy surrounding it were arranged by Aldrich whose hatred of the press and ploys to evade it had sharpened his skills of organizing sub-rosa meetings. He was fond of travel and collected art and rare books and was generally regarded as the most influential politician on Capitol Hill at the time. A Rhode Island Republican, Aldrich headed the National Monetary Commission set up to study the nation's monetary system after the panic of 1907.

The commission consisted of nine representatives and nine senators but actually was a sham since Aldrich conducted its activities the way he wanted to—in private. His penchant for travel and secrecy led him to take the commission and its advisers to Europe to confer with the elite central bankers who brainwashed him (which apparently wasn't very hard to do) and gained a powerful political ally in setting up a private central bank in the United States. The foreign bankers had sent their man, Paul Warburg, here to whip the plan into shape. Warburg was a German banker who joined the New York investment banking firm of Kuhn, Loeb & Company.

This was not the first successful attempt to set up a central bank in the United States. The attempt had been made almost from the beginning of the Republic. G. Edward Griffin in *The Creature from Jekyll Island* notes there were three central banks before the present one that was authorized by Congress (probably unconstitutionally) in 1913, including the Bank of North America, which operated briefly during the Revolutionary War. It was folded under resentment in little more than a year.

The other central banks, of course, include the one instigated and supported vigorously by Alexander Hamilton in a running constitutional feud with Thomas Jefferson. Jefferson's cousin, John Marshall, who also feuded over the meaning of the Constitution with him, ruled in favor of the bank. That ruling encompassed the all-inclusive "necessary and proper" clause of the Constitution pertaining to Congressional powers that Hamilton had argued for earlier.

The second bank owes its demise in 1836 to Andrew Jackson who labeled bankers "a den of vipers." It is interesting to note that foreigners have always owned a considerable chunk of stock in the central banks, including the Federal Reserve Bank, which they heavily financed and influenced. Some of the stock ownership by foreigners was handled by their operatives in the United States and hidden from public scrutiny. The Fed will not divulge the individual names of stock owners of the Federal Reserve banks who own the Fed stock under provisions written into the scheme at Jekyll Island by the bankers themselves. The stock is not transferable.

Besides secret meetings in Europe, Aldrich also held meetings with the bankers away from the despised press on his private yacht and other places. He had been considering a site for this secret meeting when one of the bankers suggested Jekyll Island. That was an idyllic spot six miles off the southeast corner of Georgia. The haven had been bought in 1886 by wealthy families headed by J.P. Morgan and including the Rockefellers and Vanderbilts. It was used as an exclusive hunt club and as an escape from the harsh New York winters. The families who were members of the club were estimated to represent one-sixth to one-fourth of the world's wealth at the time.

Aldrich was wealthy on his own, and that wealth had grown fabulously during his thirty-odd years in Washington. His daughter, Abby, married John D. Rockefeller Jr., making Aldrich the grandfather of the Rockefeller boys—Nelson, David, Laurance, Winthrop, and John D. III. Aldrich was a representative of the Rockefeller interests, and the Rockefellers were just as eager to get the central bank set up as were the Rothschilds. His congressional influence and his affiliation with the Rockefellers and Morgans as well as his position in the Senate gave him considerable clout. He was the key to the bankers getting their scheme, once molded into shape, through Congress, although he resigned from the Senate a short while before legislation was actually passed.

In fact, Aldrich and Frank Vanderlip, a New York banker, and other bankers lobbied against the Democratic bill in order to pretend they were against it, although it was essentially the same legislation spawned at Jekyll Island, which they wrote.

The senator was seventy at the time, and his hair, which he wore close-cropped, was scarce and white making a high forehead more prominent, according to his biographer. His handle-bar mustache, piercing eyes, and broad shoulders led to his biographer's description of him as "a fine specimen of mature vigor." He was domineering and prone to giving orders but had an urbane tone, relates Nathaniel Wright Stephenson. At this stage of his career, two things concerned him most: changing the nation's banking system to encompass a central bank and building a retirement mansion at Indian Oaks back home in his native Rhode Island.

THE COMMISSION

In making up the commission, Aldrich chose none of the congressional members such as Representative Charles A Lindberg Sr. or Senator Robert Lafollette who were fighting the so-called Bankers' Trust. He picked the members carefully but relied on just a few men: Henry P. Davison, hand-picked by J.P. Morgan; Abraham Piatt Andrew, assistant secretary of the Treasury in the Taft administration at the time and former assistant professor at Harvard; and G. M. Reynolds, president of the American Bankers Association. Davison was virtually a member of the commission. Later, Frank Vanderlip and Paul Warburg joined Davison and Andrew in the senator's inner circle of advisers. Benjamin Strong, another Morgan man, also was influential in input and helped write the legislation.

Reynolds was not included on the train trip. Others who were, according to a banker who attended, besides Aldrich and his secretary, Shelton, included Andrew, Vanderlip, president of the National City Bank of New York, the largest New York bank at the time, which represented Rockefeller oil money as well as Kuhn, Loeb, and Company; Benjamin Strong, a partner in J.P. Morgan and Company; Paul Warburg, of Kuhn, Loeb & Company, who was not even an American citizen; Davison, senior partner in J. P. Morgan; and Charles D. Norton, president of J.P. Morgan's First National Bank of New York.

Norton was a secretary to Taft, so the president probably was aware of the plan, although the bankers later dumped Taft in favor of Woodrow Wilson, who helped them win government approval for their scheme. Taft wound up as Chief Justice of the Supreme Court, not bad compensation for losing the presidency.

Taft was a fairly popular president and without the candidacy of Theodore Roosevelt on the Bull Moose ticket, which cost him votes, probably would have defeated the little known Wilson. Where Roosevelt got his money to finance his campaign is still a mystery to some historians who speculate the bankers provided it. They, like many corporations and banks still do today, covered their flank by supplying money to the campaigns of both Taft and Wilson.

The destination for the ultra-secret confab of Ben (Strong), Paul (Warburg), Abe (Andrew), Nelson or Zivil (Aldrich), Orville (Vanderlip), Wilbur (Davison), and Charles (Norton) was the Jekyll Island winter refuge. In addition to the secrecy it provided, the private retreat offered deer, wild turkeys, raccoons, hawks, egrets, herons, shore birds, and other wildlife for hunting as well as both freshwater and ocean fishing.

Thanks to warm ocean currents, Jekyll Island provided the weather for outdoor activity in November, but hunting game was not the object of the rich bankers on this trip. The money and credit of the United States and a banking monopoly protected by the government was their prey. They planned to work overtime to devise a way to get it. Although they feared publicity, they had no threat from police or the FBI as the Mafia faced at a secret gathering in upstate New York shortly after World War II. In terms of the take, their crime, however, dwarfed all the Mafia's ill-gotten gains before or since.

In order to get the island ready for Aldrich's group, extraordinary precautions were taken to secure secrecy. In addition to those used on the New York end of the journey, even more elaborate precautions were taken at Jekyll. All the hired help on the island received a two-week vacation. New servants were brought in from the mainland. The new help wouldn't recognize any of the bankers attending the meeting, and they would only hear them refer to each other by their first or fictitious names.

ALL ABOARD

As soon as the bankers were safely aboard the train, they lost no time and went straight to work. It had been two years since the commission was founded, and it had been running up a hefty tab (about three hundred thousand dollars) with nothing to show for it. Aldrich badly needed a written proposal. Although the commission was supposed to have been open and represented by members of both houses, Aldrich dominated it. The senator needed a plan for currency reform, a central bank to his way of thinking—something in writing—something he could take public and later present to Congress. Unfortunately for the public, the bankers got to write their own plan with Aldrich's input, especially from the standpoint of what was politically feasible.

Haggling on how to accomplish this task and what to include and exclude surfaced among the bankers immediately. Everyone, wrote Vanderlip, had a pet proposal, although they agreed with the overall objective. Finally, Vanderlip, a former economics writer, recalls in his autobiography *From Farm Boy to Financier* that amid the suggestions and objections, he offered a plan: "to set down those things about which we are agreed; then, one by one, we can take up those things about which we seem to disagree." The plan was accepted, and for his trouble, Vanderlip was made secretary.

The men who would spend almost a fortnight together in close quarters either conferring, dining, or socializing were mostly of middle-class backgrounds. They had, however, worked themselves into positions where they represented vast wealth and power and some of the most influential men in the world. In short, they were the technicians and minions for the super rich.

Problems, some technical and others political or administrative, that had to be worked out at Jekyll included whether there would be a uniform discount rate or regional rates; how to secure a more elastic or flexible (expanding and contracting) currency; whether there should be one central bank or more for political reasons to house the nation's bank reserves scattered in banks throughout the country; the way members would be selected and by whom and who would have power to remove them; whether ownership of stock would be by private bankers, government, or a partnership of both; and how to disguise the plan so that it could be sold to Congress and the nation.

Other matters to be decided included how to shift any losses from the owners of the banks to the taxpayers and also how to gain control of all banks, small and large. In other words, they wanted to create a monopoly.

Aldrich and his entourage moved immediately to the rear room of his private car and began work as soon as the train started moving. From accounts pieced together from biographies, autobiographies of the participants, and historical accounts and congressional reports since that time, the conversation could have gone something like this:

CHAPTER II

ABOARD THE TRAIN

Zivil: Gentlemen, I'm glad to see that you all arrived safely and, I hope, unnoticed by anyone. I apologize for the strict secrecy measures I had to ask you to follow, but I think you all know how important it is that our mission not be reported by the press. I understand some of you went to a lot of trouble to disguise yourselves.

Wilbur (Davison): Yes, sir, Zivil. You should have seen Paul [Warburg] with his shotgun and hunting outfit. You surely would have taken him for a true Georgia sharpshooter. (Laughter.)

Zivil: I'll bet he couldn't hit a barn. But we must get to work. As you all know, it has been some time now since President [Theodore] Roosevelt signed the bill creating the Monetary Commission to study the American banking system. As chairman of the Senate Finance Committee as well as the Monetary Commission, I have, with some of you in attendance, met with the heads of Europe's largest banks during that time, and we have studied their systems. As a matter of fact, we have one of their experts, Mr. War... er...Paul, that is, with us now as a partner of Kuhn, Loeb &

Company. Although he is not yet an American citizen, he is an adviser to this panel because of his European banking background. I hope he can help us come up with a central bank model after those of Europe, England or Germany maybe, that will control all banks and the currency of the United States.

As you know, it is imperative that I come up with a plan in legislative form soon to present to Congress, and one that will meet the approval of the American people who, at this juncture, are not overly fond of bankers, and New York bankers like you in particular. (Laughter.)

Therefore, we must keep this meeting secret and disguise this plan to meet public approval as much as possible and still set up a central banking system, pardon the term, as well. There are many other problems we must solve to make the plan palatable.

So, you can see we have a lot of work to do during the next week or ten days at Jekyll Island. For once we leave there, it will be almost impossible to again have the secrecy and seclusion needed to get the job done without the watchful eyes of Congress and the prying press. I thank you all for coming.

(There is some commotion with several members shouting for attention. Finally, Benjamin Strong [Ben], a partner in J.P. Morgan and Company, emerges as the speaker as other voices trail off. Strong would later become president of the New York Federal Reserve Board and have much to do with the monetary policy that led to the Great Depression.)

Ben: Zivil, I submit that this legislation should call for the establishment of one central bank with an elastic currency that can expand and contract as conditions warrant. The system should be run by bankers, and it should be headquartered in New York—the nation's largest financial center. I also believe the notes to be issued under the new system should be obligations of the banks and not the U.S. government.

Paul (Warburg): (in his thick German accent that irritated some of those present despite his quiet, mild manner) Zivil, as you well know, I have long been promoting a central bank and have spoken and written much to annunciate the idea. But we must not call it by that name or let the public suspect that we are setting up a central bank at all. In fact, we must disguise it so that the public will not suspect it is a central bank. We could call it by some federal name, like the Federal Reserve System, as an example, although it would not, of course, be federal.

I disagree with my friend, Ben, and think the banks' notes should most certainly be obligations of the U.S. government. The burden of any bank losses should be shifted from the banks to the United States government. I also think the European systems should be disguised somewhat to take into account American political concerns.

Zivil (Aldrich): I think I know more about American political concerns than you do, Mr. Warbu…, I mean, Paul, and what the American people and Congress will and will not accept. Whatever form the plan for a consolidated bank takes, it should be kept as free of politics as possible—and that means Congress should not appoint the directors or perform any administrative functions relating to the system. But that, of course, raises the question of how we do this since the Constitution expressly gives the power to Congress to borrow money on the credit of the United States and to coin money and regulate its value.

You can bet there will be an argument about that. But to counter it, we have John Marshall's ruling that was also used by Alexander Hamilton that Congress has a right to make laws "necessary and proper" for carrying out all of its powers not expressly spelled out in the Constitution.

We must also remember that the Constitution does not delegate powers to the federal government to issue bills of credit. This may not become an issue, but if it does, we can use Alexander Hamilton's argument to support our position or maybe propose a constitutional amendment, if necessary.

Paul: If I may interject...

Zivil: I suspected you might.

Wilbur (Davison): (always eager to prevent any personal clashes) I wish I had something to interject on that problem myself. (Laughter.)

Paul: We might have Congress control the bank in name only by setting up a board of directors but having a majority of them chosen by the banks. On the other point, even if we do have several regional banks for public and congressional window dressing, the bank would actually still be run from New York. That would placate the public into believing the regions were getting equal treatment when actually the New York bank would be making the decisions.

Zivil: But again, I insist, congressional politics must be kept out of it.

Paul: Then we may devise a plan to shift some of the responsibility, especially the appointment of the administrators, to the president but keep the real work of the board in the hands of bankers.

Wilbur (Davison): Makes sense, even though that would be slightly unconstitutional and may be difficult to convince Congress. (Grinning.) There also is strong sentiment in the country against corporate monopolies, which, in effect, is what we would be creating. This is going to be a difficult sell because of the strong sentiment against corporate monopolies and legislation such as the Sherman Antitrust Act to control them. But I think we can pull it off.

Zivil: You're right, Henry. I agree with what you say.

Ben: I would like to stress again my very strong objections to having the Federal Reserve notes be obligations of the United States. I think that could spell disaster for the country some day.

Orville (Vanderlip): Gentlemen, I think this would be a good place for me to cite some very sage advice I once received from a friend, Frank Trumbull, chairman of the Chesapeake and Ohio Railway. Mr. Trumbull suggested that we ought to first set down the things about which we are agreed. Then, one by one, take up those things about which we seem to be disagreed. (Applause.)

Wilbur: I sense some agreement here. Mr. Chairman, I make a motion that we make Orville [Vanderlip] our amanuensis, since he is a writer and also knows shorthand.

Zivil: Any objections? (Pause.) So be it.

Orville: (taking up pad) We all, I think, are agreed we have to have a more elastic currency through a bank or banks, that will hold the reserves of all the banks. We also want the system kept out of politics and for bankers to have the most, if not total, control. We will, of course, have to decide how we can gain total private ownership or let the government own no stock or as little as we can get away with and how we can keep Congress out of it and get around the Constitution in so doing, whether it should be only one bank or contain several regional banks. How the discount rate will work also will be of concern. Will it be uniform or vary by region? In addition, what open-market operations should we be engaged in, and should the services of the system be restricted to banks?

Zivil: As you can see, gentlemen, it will take all of our time at Jekyll Island to work these matters into an acceptable form for Congress. And, even then, we will have a lot of propaganda work to do to sell the plan. But I can tell you I am unalterably opposed to more than one discount rate. This would lead to grave charges by the public and some congressmen of banker control from New York. One discount rate, even if surreptitiously set from New York, would be better, I think.

IDENTITY THREATENED

The plotters worked late into the night and started again early the next morning. As the train reached Brunswick, Georgia, a town of about three thousand people, where the bankers would depart by boat for Jekyll Island, the stationmaster almost blew their cover. He entered the private car and revealed that he knew their identities. Davison quickly whisked him outside ostensibly to give him the true story. He was led to join a few local reporters from a weekly newspaper who were seen on the platform.

Davison, who knew them from previous hunting trips, chatted briefly with them and the stationmaster, and they immediately dispersed. It never has been historically established what precisely Davison (Wilbur) said to the reporters. The best guess is that he persuaded them it was nothing more than a holiday (Thanksgiving) hunting outing at the Jekyll Island Hunt Club.

Nathaniel Wright, in his biography of Aldrich, says Davison was asked what he told the reporters but that he never volunteered the information. In any event, it is logical to assume that Davison never told them the truth, and the local reporters bought whatever story he told them since the secret meeting or its purpose was not uncovered.

After arriving at Jekyll, the party met in the clubhouse, which was, as Vanderlip (Orville) relates it, "built for people with a taste for luxury." He adds some color (p. 216):

"The live-oak trees wear fantastic beards of Spanish moss on Jekyll Island; in November brown leaves make its forests utterly charming. Without our ever stopping to hunt, deer, turkey and quail appeared on the table; there were pans of oysters not an hour old when they were scalloped; there were country hams with that incomparable flavor that is given to them in the South. We were working ...morning, noon and night, and ate enormously." For Thanksgiving, he adds, "We ate wild turkey with oyster stuffing and went right back to work."

After a week of work, when the conferees had agreed on the draft of a plan, it was decided to take a day off and go duck hunting. "I shall never forget [Davison] Wilbur as he came down the next morning, ready for the sport, with all the physical vitality bursting forth that had been cooped up during a week of ceaseless mental strain," Paul (Warburg) relates (p. 100) in Davison's biography by Thomas W. Lamont.

Warburg himself was said by his son to have looked ridiculous disguising himself as a hunter when boarding the train in New Jersey. James Warburg wrote that his father never owned and knew little about shotguns but borrowed one for the occasion (*The Creature from Jekyll Island*, p. 10).

The bankers got the essentials of what they wanted at Jekyll Island but left some details to be wrapped up administratively so as not to jolt the public too much. Although they did not ultimately get everything they wanted in the final act passed by Congress, they deliberately worded it so vaguely that they were able to accomplish much in their administration of the legislation.

The final draft was known as the Aldrich Plan, although Democrats denounced it for political reasons in the 1912 election and came up with another, the Federal Reserve Act, which was essentially the same.

DUBIOUS PASSAGE

Aldrich retired from the Senate before the final act was passed, and Woodrow Wilson defeated Taft with the help of Teddy Roosevelt. The final bill was enacted under dubious circumstances during the Christmas holiday season in 1913. It would be two years and long after congressional leaders underhandedly maneuvered to pass the bill for Wilson's signature before any news that the Jekyll Island secret meeting took place. Even then, the story by B.C. Forbes was given little credence by the leaders who should have been astounded, as Eustice Mullins, who did one of the first books on the secret founding, observed. Forbes wrote:

> Picture a party of the nation's greatest bankers stealing out of New York on a private railroad car under cover of darkness, stealthily hieing hundreds of miles south, embarking on a mysterious launch, sneaking onto an island deserted by all but a few servants, living there a full week under such rigid secrecy that the names of not one of them was once mentioned lest the

servants learn their identity and disclose to the world
this strangest, most secret expedition in the history of
American finance. I am not romancing; I am giving
to the world, for the first time, the real story of how
the famous Aldrich currency report, the foundation
of our new currency system, was written...

The final bill that passed under sub-rosa manipulation
called for an elastic currency and a privately owned bank that
included twelve regions as a disguise for New York banker
control, a uniform discount rate, removal of the system from
congressional control by having the administrators appointed
by the president and not Congress. This, of course, is another
reason it was unconstitutional from the start. The bill also
called for making the notes of the bank obligations of the
United States and not the banks. Davison and Warburg had
convinced Strong to change his mind. Since the bank was
a bank of issue, it also meant that the nation's money and
credit had been handed over to a group of private bankers—an
unconstitutional act that has never been tested in the Supreme
Court.

The law has been twice amended since 1913, but it is
essentially the same except for giving more authority to
the Board of Governors who are political appointees of the
president's. Most of the Fed chairmen, such as Alan Greenspan,
Paul Volcker, and William McChesney Martin as examples,
have also been members of the Council on Foreign Relations
(CFR), an elite group that has controlled U.S. foreign policy
for almost a century. It doesn't matter which party is in power,
the elites always get their man in charge of the Fed, and he
most always swings the door in from Wall Street.

Some presidents have secretly or openly challenged the
Fed's legality and independence as have some congressmen
and senators through the ninety-plus years of its existence. But
the intermittent fury and threats all have died down, and the
Fed has continued with few changes. Its chairmen know that

if push comes to shove, they have the money and the power behind them to stay in business, even though they may bend a little to avoid public outrage.

Is the Fed biased in favor of banks and elite holders of most of the nation's wealth? Even though his reporting confirms this, Grieder defends the Fed system and the technocrats that run it as acting in good faith but just not always getting it right because of incomprehensible, complicated economic factors. If that's so, why is it that the decisions never come out in favor of farmers, laborers, and other wage earners instead of bankers and holders of most of the nation's wealth?

After all, even Volker and Greenspan have let it clearly be known who their constituents are and have acted accordingly.

SECRET RETURN

There was no Bertie Forbes to record it, but following the meeting at Jekyll Island, the group returned north "as secretly as we had gone south" (p. 217), Frank Vanderlip related. Aldrich and Andrew left the train at Washington while Warburg, Davison, Strong, and Vanderlip went on to New York, but not for long. Congress was about to meet, and Aldrich became ill before, as Vanderlip put it, writing "an appropriate document to accompany his plan." So, Strong and Vanderlip were summoned to Washington to prepare the report. That meant the legislation was of, by, and for the bankers, since the bankers planned and wrote it. Although the Aldrich plan was defeated, its essential points were in the bill that finally passed under the name of the Federal Reserve Act.

It would be three years following the conclave at Jekyll, plus a change in presidential administrations before the bankers could finally see their handiwork completed. In the interim, they still had a lot of selling to do to the public and Congress.

So, they set up a five-million-dollar slush fund for a nationwide propaganda campaign to support the Jekyll Island plan. They used professors from the Rockefeller-endowed University of Chicago and Harvard, which also got its fair share of funding from Rockefeller dollars, and Princeton, where Woodrow Wilson was former president, to spread favorable news about the plan.

It is unfortunate that David Rockefeller in his *David Rockefeller—Memoirs* failed to shed any light on Aldrich's involvement in the Federal Reserve conspiracy. He must have been privy to much of his maternal grandfather's involvement in the plot. But except for a brief reference to Aldrich and the fact he was instrumental in the Fed's formation, he skips the subject entirely. He does confirm he "suggested" Paul Volcker to Jimmy Carter for chairman of the Federal Reserve, and also that he, Rockefeller, could have become, at different times, either secretary of the Treasury or Fed chairman himself.

CHAPTER III

OPPONENTS

One of the main opponents of the establishment of the private central bank—or the money trust, as he called it—was Charles A. Lindbergh Sr., a Minnesota congressman. Another was Sen. Robert M. LaFollette, whose opposition, he said, cost him the presidency. Lindbergh, with opposition from the *New York Times* and the bankers, had his political career destroyed.

But before it was, largely as the result of his outcry, Congress appointed a subcommittee (the Pugo Committee) of the House Banking and Currency Committee to investigate the control of money and credit in the United States. The deck was stacked when Samuel Untermyer, a wealthy New York corporate lawyer, was appointed to conduct the investigation. Untermyer controlled the questioning of bankers, prolonged the hearings, and issued a lengthy and almost incomprehensible report of droning uninformative testimony. He never even bothered to call the two men most responsible for the investigation in the first place: Lindbergh and LaFollette.

When the final bill (known in the House as "the Glass Bill") was presented to the conference committee on December 22, 1913, Lindbergh in a floor speech exclaimed (p. 165 of *Lindbergh of Minnesota* by Bruce Larson, Harcourt Brace

23

Jovanovich Jr., New York): It "...establishes the most gigantic trust on earth...When the president signs this act, the invisible government by the money power, proven to exist by the Money Trust investigation, will be legalized." This is a "Christmas present to the Money Trust."

In the election of 1912, former President Theodore Roosevelt ran as a third party candidate against William Howard Taft and secured enough Republican votes to elect Woodrow Wilson, a little known governor of New Jersey. What was the source of all the money for Roosevelt's campaign, and why did he make the move? That is still a mystery to some historians.

Eustice Mullins in *The Secrets of the Federal Reserve* states that the bankers supported all three candidates but thought that Wilson, his unofficial adviser, Colonel Edward Mandel House, and the Democrats could deliver on the central bank plan and doubted that Taft, a Republican, could. In any event, that's what happened. Wilson also got an income tax plan passed. Colonel Edward Mandel House (he was no colonel) was reputed to be a front for the Rothschild banking family of England and was a close adviser to President Wilson. He was instrumental in influencing Wilson to support the legislation that set up the central bank.

The Republican Convention in 1912 supported the Aldrich Plan, but the Democrats abandoned it in support of the Federal Reserve Act. Both bills were fundamentally identical, although they differed somewhat in form and control.

THE PEOPLE PAY

On the point of whether the bank notes were to be obligations of the United States or the Federal Reserve, Warburg was adamant. President Wilson said he had to compromise on this point to get the legislation through Congress. Warburg and Davison had taken Strong, who became the first chairman of the controlling Federal Reserve Bank of New York, aside and convinced him to change his mind. Strong, who had been just as stern about not having the notes U.S. obligations, said after the meeting that it didn't really matter who had the note obligation. If it had gone the other way, the United States might not be holding more than eight trillion dollars worth of debt on which the bankers get more than their fair share of interest plus their Fed stock dividends.

The Federal Reserve Act was finally passed on December 23, 1913. Mullins wrote (p. 29): "History proved that on that day, the Constitution ceased to be the governing covenant of the American people, and our liberties were handed over to a small group of international bankers," just as presidents Jefferson, Lincoln, Jackson, and Garfield had warned.

In *The Federal Reserve Conspiracy*, Antony C. Sutton relates in detail the machinations that went on in Congress during the week leading up to passage of the Federal Reserve Act. He calls it "...one of the more disgraceful unconstitutional perversions of political power in American history." As an example, the House-Senate conferees who had to agree on twenty to forty differences in their versions of the bill excluded all Republican members. Both Senator Robert L. Owen and Representative Carter Glass, who had charge of the bills in their respective chambers, were bankers and, therefore, had conflicts of interest. The speediness with which the bill was rushed through Congress was never before or after equaled in Congress, Sutton declares, and it "...is ominously comparable to the rubber stamp lawmaking of banana republics." Sutton also warned:

"Quietly, without fanfare—and with the vast bulk of citizens unaware—the world bankers have been building an international money machine: an international Federal Reserve System with the power to control the world's financial and economic systems."

One need only look at the Fed's record to see the system has been a dismal failure by any standard.

Its stated objective was to stabilize the economy and prevent bank panics. The late Chairman William McChesney Martin once even stated it also was to protect the value of the dollar. Well, the purchasing power of the dollar has been reduced to less than a dime since 1914, and the economy has been through booms and busts and is anything but stable. But then, as G. Edward Griffin, in *The Creature from Jekyll Island* (American Media, Westlake Village, California) points out, the stated objective was phony from the start and for the public's consumption only.

After gaining control of the nation's credit and money, the Fed was able to artificially create fiat money. The private bank with the government's backing took no risk, and its phony money was made legal tender. The Fed has been accused of creating wars and inflation by expanding or contracting the money supply. Its fiat money financed World Wars I and II and all those in between and plus the Cold War and Bosnia-Herzegovnia, Sudan/Afganistan, and Iraq.

Mullins contends World War I could not have occurred without the Fed financing of Germany, because it was too broke to fight a war. Griffin points out that the Fed has presided over stock market crashes in 1921 and 1929 plus the ten-year Great Depression and five recessions. Add to this the fact that the United States has become a huge debtor nation under the Fed's guidance and is racking up record trade and budget deficits.

Griffin calls for the abolition of the Federal Reserve System for several reasons including "it cannot stabilize the economy; and it encourages war, destabilizes the economy and is an instrument of totalitarianism."

The decline of the dollar, the astronomical debt burden thrust on the American people, recessions, and the Great Depression and other offenses against the American people since the founding of the Federal Reserve Board have been well documented in various books, newspapers, and other publications.

Speaking of the national debt, which is officially listed at about eight trillion dollars, no one really knows the exact figure. It may be above forty trillion dollars, and the Treasury Department certainly could not pay if all outstanding bonds were presented for payment. Al Martin, who wrote *The Conspirators*, which detailed the Iran-Contra scams, writes on his Web site, Al Martin Raw, of a scam from 1984 to 1988 in which non-recorded U.S. Treasury instruments were allegedly issued and funded by the Federal Reserve Board.

He doesn't know if the Fed was involved because the secretary of the Treasury has power to issue the bonds, and Martin said this was done. They were issued to a concern set up for the purpose, which used the bonds as assets to commit a fraud, according to Martin. The trick, according to him, was to make sure the bonds would never be drawn on and would be rolled over when the time of their expiration approached.

Martin quotes former Treasury Secretary Paul O'Neill as saying, "We don't know where the debt is. That's why we don't know what the national debt of the United States is."

CHAPTER IV

MYSTERIOUS HAPPENINGS

From a human life and career standpoint, there also have been mysterious occurrences that some historians attribute directly to the so-called "money trust." They include:

The attempted assassination of Andrew Jackson, who vetoed renewal of the charter of the Bank of the United States in 1832 and instigated the removal of government deposits from the bank, which he transferred to state banks. Griffin (p. 357) quotes a source as relating that the would-be assassin, Richard Lawrence, who pleaded insanity, later bragged that powerful Europeans promised him protection.

The assassination of Abraham Lincoln, which some historians link to his issuance of "Greenbacks" that bore no interest and were backed by the government's credit. This way, Lincoln avoided borrowing from large New York banks at exorbitant interest rates to pay for Civil War debts. Lincoln also was a staunch opponent of private bankers who were trying to gain control of the nation's money and credit.

James Garfield also opposed private control of United States currency and expounded his position shortly before his assassination.

Other presidents who have challenged the independent Fed included Ronald Reagan and John F. Kennedy, Richard

Nixon and Gerald Ford. The latter two were obstacles to Nelson Rockefeller's desire to be president. Some writers have linked Nixon's ousting and Ford's attempted assassinations to this fact. The jury is still out on Kennedy, who failed to toe the line of the shadow government as did Reagan, although both had top posts in their administrations manned by members of organizations involved in controlling foreign policy—the Council on Foreign Relations, the Trilateral Commission, and the Order of Skull and Bones, as examples.

Congressman Charles A. Lindbergh, father of the famous aviator, offered an impeachment resolution against the members of the Federal Reserve Board four years after the Fed was formed, but the resolution was never acted upon. Lindbergh was a constant critic of the "money trust," and for his efforts, he drew heavy criticism from the *New York Times* and contributions to his political opponents by the money trust. He was defeated in bids to return to Congress and to become governor of Minnesota. He said the Federal Reserve Act would "...establish the most gigantic trust on earth." While Lindberg was running for governor of Minnesota, federal government agents destroyed his book, *Why Is Your Country at War,* along with the original plates of the book. The book attacked the "money trust" and its part in promoting World War I.

Lindbergh told Congress that the Glass Bill—the House's final version of the Federal Reserve bill—would "...incorporate, canonize, and sanctify a private monopoly of the money and credit of the nation....It violates every principle of popular, democratic, representative government and every declaration of the Democratic Party and platform pledges from Thomas Jefferson down to the beginning of this Congress" (quoted by Bruce Larson in *Lindbergh of Minnesota*, p. 161). Lindbergh made a statement to the House (p. 215) in 1916 that may be just as applicable today as then: "The plain truth is that neither of these great parties, as at present led and manipulated by an invisible government, is fit to manage the destinies of a great people…"

Senator Robert LaFollette also was a fierce opponent of the "money trust" and charged that just a few men were controlling the United States. He claimed that his public opposition to the "Bankers' Trust" cost him the presidency of the United States. Very few voices are heard in Congress in opposition to the Fed, which is still plunging the nation more and more into debt. Opponents of the Fed are disparaged and made to look like crackpots, because they go against the system.

PATMAN'S WARNING

The late Wright Patman, chairman of the House Banking and Currency Committee for a decade during the sixties and seventies, is a good example. The controlled media ignored his warnings against "the international banking cartel" that he claimed made an accounting to no one. Not even the General Accounting Office, watchdog of Congress, has jurisdiction over the Fed. There have been recent audits relating to expenses and expenditures in the operation but still no in-depth studies of stock ownership, profits, and secret affiliations and conversations and dealings with foreign banks or governments.

Patman's voice went largely unheard, and that appears to be the fate of another Texan—Congressman Ron Paul—who has introduced bills to audit the Fed as well as to repeal the Federal Reserve Act of 1913 to no avail.

Incidentally, the Republican State Platform Committee in 1998 and again in 2000 called for the abolition of the Fed and also a congressional audit of it. President George W. Bush ignored the platform, which was written by grassroots Texas Republicans, in his quest for the presidency.

Bush has already made several appointments to the seven-member Federal Reserve Board including Donald Kohn, former chief secretary and economist at the central bank and considered Alan Greenspan's right-hand man. He also nominated Greenspan for still another term as chairman and will also appoint his successor.

Actually, Greenspan's latest appointment was for only two years since his tenure as a Fed governor expired before he could serve it out. There was a lot of speculation about why Bush made the early announcement of the nomination, which Greenspan quickly said he would accept in a statement of clarity, which is uncommon for the flimflam man. Greenspan supported Bush's tax cuts, and Bush counted on him again with other proposed tax cuts.

ANOTHER IMPEACHMENT ATTEMPT

About a couple of decades after Lindbergh tried to impeach the Federal Reserve Board and others, Congressman Louis T. McFadden, chairman of the House Banking and Currency Committee, also attempted it. McFadden named Herbert Hoover and the Federal Reserve Board of Governors for their alleged part in the Great Depression. They included Eugene Meyer, father of Katherine Graham, late director of the *Washington Post* who said in her book, *Personal History* (p. 56), that Meyer was just trying to turn about the Depression. Some historians charge he was part of the money trust that caused it.

McFadden suffered two attempts on his life and died mysteriously in 1936 while on a visit to New York. The *New York Times*, a critic of McFadden and friend of bankers and Wall Street, reported the death as coronary thrombosis. About the two previous attempts on his life, Citizens Against Banksters quoted from *Pelley's Weekly* of October 14, 1936, a day after McFadden's sudden death, "The first attack came in the form of two revolver shots fired at him from ambush as he was alighting from a car in front of one of the Capital hotels." The bullets missed but buried themselves in the car's structure, the story said. As for the other attempt, it reported, "He became violently ill after partaking of food at a political banquet..." in Washington. It went on to relate that a physician at the banquet procured a stomach pump and performed emergency treatment.

In his caustic comments in attempting to impeach Hoover and the Federal Reserve Board members on June 10, 1932, McFadden said (*Collected Speeches of Louis T. McFadden, Congressional Records*, p. 298):

"Mr. Chairman, we have in this country one of the most corrupt institutions the world has ever known. I refer to the Federal Reserve Board and the Federal Reserve banks. The Federal Reserve Board has cheated the Government of the United States and the people of the United States out of enough money to pay the national debt..."

There is another incident relating to a former chairman of the House Banking committee—Representative Henry Gonzalez (D-Texas), a frequent critic of the Fed. According to Al Martin Raw, Gonzalez's car was machine-gunned in front of the townhouse he owned in Washington. Martin thinks it was related to the congressman's attempt to obtain information in the Iran-Contra scandal, although Gonzalez also tried to pry information about the operations of the Fed.

The sad part of the overall story is that Congress has abdicated its constitutional authority and handed it over to private bankers. "No authority has ever been given to create a central bank," Congressman Paul charges. But the Federal Reserve Act of 1913 has never been constitutionally challenged in court.

There is another side to the story. Even the Fed and the Treasury Department are giving way to the International Monetary Fund while Congress—the only body that has the constitutional responsibility for controlling and guaranteeing the value of the currency—adopts the role of a bystander.

"Congress no longer takes any control or authority over the *de facto* monetary system. It has all been transferred to the IMF (International Monetary Fund) and World Bank..." John Prukof, legal researcher, wrote in *The Free Press* (3/98 issue). It should be emphasized, however, that Congress still has power to abolish the Fed and re-assume its constitutional responsibilities. Only an irate public can see that that happens. Even then, the money supporters of the Fed have such power that it probably could never be done.

President Franklin Roosevelt seized the people's gold under the Emergency Banking Act of 1933, and he used an executive order under the Emergency War Powers Act of 1933 to nationalize silver in 1934. Because of these two and subsequent actions, fiat U.S. money is backed by nothing but the property of the people such as home mortgages. "The American people and their property are in a state of permanent bondage," concludes Dr. Eugene Schroder in *Constitution: Fact or Fiction* (Buffalo Creek Press, Cleburne, Texas).

CHAPTER V

GREENSPAN AND THE PRESS

The latest long-term Fed chairman, Alan Greenspan, was a former private economic consultant for the elite bankers that control the Federal Reserve Board. His affiliations included major Wall Street firms such as J.P. Morgan and Company, Morgan Guaranty Trust, the Dreyfus Fund, and others.

Arguably, the Fed chairman who answers to no one and obfuscates his actions before Congress is about as powerful as the president. Yet Greenspan served eighteen years in office to the president's maximum of eight. It all indicates that the elites have solid control of the Federal Reserve System as well as foreign policy. Greenspan, a member of the Council on Foreign Relations (CFR), let the country know in June 1999 that he needed no concrete proof of inflation to raise interest rates. All he has to do is suspect it. He also admitted that he doesn't understand some of the new technological changes in the economy. That doesn't matter either.

The old figures-cruncher had the press tagging along for his every convoluted phrase and has even sold them on the Fed's constitutional legitimacy. As an example, Bob Woodward, in his book *Maestro*, which is largely an exaltation of Greenspan's performance as the title implies, states this about Fed appointments:

"Under the law and the Constitution, the President makes the appointments to the (Federal Reserve) Board, and the Senate confirms them." The Constitution does not mention a central bank, and the founding fathers were adamantly opposed to one much less stating how appointments should be made to such a bank. The power to appoint was usurped from Congress under the Jekyll Island plan written by the bankers and later passed by Congress under furtive circumstances.

It is interesting that Woodward and Grieder, both at the *Post* during much of the late Katherine Graham's reign, never bothered to look into the background of her father, Eugene Meyer, chairman of the Fed during Herbert Hoover's presidency. Grieder does make one mention of him and depicts him as trying to get more money into the system to stem the recession.

In her *Personal History*, Ms. Graham mentions (p. 56) how overworked Meyer was as Fed chairman "in an attempt to turn about the Depression" and added that he "conceptualized the Reconstruction Finance Corporation" and "...guided the banking and monetary policies of the United States domestically and abroad."

Mullins tells us (p. 99) that there were "...revelations of duplications of hundreds of millions of dollars worth of bonds during Meyer's directorship of the War Finance Corporation, the alteration of the books during a congressional investigation, and that Meyer came out of the situation with many millions of dollars with which he bought a controlling interest in Allied Chemical Corporation (and) the *Washington Post*. Meyer also got to edit his testimony before it went into the *Congressional Record*, according to Mullins.

The *Post* was a struggling concern with debts of six hundred thousand dollars at the time Meyer bought it, and he was not noted for purchasing decrepit business properties. Media control to sway public opinion appears to be the true motive for the purchase. Recall that the *New York Times* already had been purchased with J.P. Morgan support, apparently for the same reason.

Ms. Graham related that Meyer wanted people on the economic staff from the London School of Economics, which Grieder referred to as the graduate school of banking and which Griffin called "the Fabian London (socialist) School of Economics."

Mullins relates that Meyer was associated with the international banking house of Lazard Freres of which his brother-in-law, George Blumenthal, and his father were partners in the Paris and London branches. Lazard Freres dealt in imports and exports of gold—the movement of which was one of the functions of the Federal Reserve System at the time.

Congressman Louis McFadden charged in a House speech that Meyer represented the Rothschild banking interests and was a liaison officer between the French Government and J.P. Morgan, also a Rothschild front.

So, the checkered past of Meyer should have offered the *Washington Post* boys lots of material for a book. But Ms. Graham may not have been too supportive of such an endeavor if the facts were bared about her father's dealings.

MORE ABOUT THE MONEY GURU

Greenspan claims to support a return to the gold standard instead of the fiat money system we now have. He probably knows better than anyone else that this will never happen. Whether he is grandstanding or not appears to be a legitimate concern in light of his positions as Fed chairman which favored the banks and Wall Street. His bugbear has always been inflation, rather than employment and the welfare of the middle class.

So, how well has he rode herd on inflation since he became Fed chairman in 1987? Robert J. Fransconi, a

Pennsylvanian, did some figuring and revealed his figures in a letter to WorldNetDaily. Using the government's Consumer Price Index, whose accuracy Greenspan has challenged as overstating inflation, Fransconi concluded the dollar lost seventy-two percent of its purchasing power during Greenspan's chairmanship. Using the same calculator, he found that the purchasing power of the dollar has declined to a nickel since the Fed was created in 1913.

One of Greenspan's biggest public relations blunders occurred on this very subject when he told a reporter who asked about suffering as a result of a weak economy that no one suffered more than stockbrokers. That was interpreted by the media as being insensitive to the suffering of the common working man. So, we know who Greenspan's constituents are, but Paul Volker topped him for arrogance. He told a complaining group of legislators from farm states pleading for easier money, "Your constituents are unhappy, mine (bond holders and bankers) aren't" (Grieder, p. 676).

Another seemingly incongruous statement by Greenspan was his testimony before the Senate Banking committee that he believes the Fed, along with other agencies, should have an expiration date.

The gold standard would negate the need for the Fed and fiat money as well as the Fed chairman's job. So, his position in light of his Wall Street background is puzzling, if it is sincere. And one cannot overlook the fact that the old economic guru takes delight in trying to cloud his testimony before Congress.

As for his background, Mullins points out (*Secrets of the Federal Reserve*, p.188) that "as a partner of J.P. Morgan Company since 1977, Greenspan represented the unbroken line of control of the Federal Reserve System by the firms represented at...Jekyll Island in 1910." Remember the J.P. Morgan representatives who helped draft the Federal Reserve

Act—Henry P. Davison and Benjamin Strong both from J.P. Morgan?

Several books have been written about Greenspan recently, and all have been complimentary of his Fed tenure and almost deify the old atheist. That's partly because the economy experienced its longest expansion in history on his watch. But whether the length of the expansion was caused by the high tech explosion and increased productivity or other factors is open to further study.

However astute he is at crunching numbers, Greenspan is just one of many economists in Washington and throughout the country. His views carry more weight because he controls the money. No one is indispensable, however, with the possible exception of Franklin Roosevelt, who obviously thought he was. The country will survive after Greenspan.

The bigger question is whether the Fed is giving way to the International Monetary Fund (IMF) or some other form of a world central bank. And, if not, whether its tools are adequate in the new technological age of instant transfers of funds in the global economy to rein the economy in or out as the Fed deems it necessary in the interest of its banker supporters.

CHAPTER VI

WHO OWNS THE FED?

There is one mysterious question that the Fed tries to get around and be indirect about even to congressmen who try to get the answer, and that is: "Who owns the Federal Reserve Board?" The U.S. government doesn't own any stock in it, although it is obligated for its notes.

Some people confuse the ownership of the Fed and the ownership of the national debt. The twelve Federal Reserve banks own the Federal Reserve Bank's stock, and individuals own stock in the Fed banks. The Federal Reserve Banks own only a small amount of the national debt but enough for a sizable profit. They own all they can handle or care to purchase. In addition, the Fed gets handling fees, controls the money supply and interest rates, and its member bank owners collect dividends on their Fed stock. In short, the Fed owners are making out all right even if they don't have the whole enchilada. The government (people) gets the debt plus interest and provides police power and a collection agency (IRS) for the Fed operations.

Eustice Mullins claims that descendents of the families that bought the original stock in the Fed still own it. It is not for sale and ordinary citizens cannot buy it, although they can, of course, buy government securities. Through the merger of banks over the years, the Fed stock has become even more concentrated among the big banks and their shareholders. It was set up that way by the jackals at Jekyll who devised the legislation.

Ever since its origin, the Fed has attempted to mislead the public as to its true operation and to keep certain information secret. Scholars and journalists still have difficulty getting information about the ownership and inside operation of the Fed, and there is an ongoing argument about it. Click on Google, and you will find that the arguments concerning the Fed get heated and involve name-calling at times.

Even noted historians don't always cut through the confusion when recounting activities of the nation's money management monopoly. That's partly because Fed spokesmen from Alan Greenspan on down try to obfuscate the actions and purpose of the institution that controls the people's money. Here's an example: In his book *A History of the American People*, Paul Johnson writes that President Andrew Jackson distrusted the government's counting of the gold stored in the vaults at Fort Knox, Kentucky.

"He [Jackson] thereby inaugurated an American tradition which continues to this day: Every year the Daughters of the American Revolution (DAR) send a committee of ladies to visit the vaults of Fort Knox to ensure that America's gold is still in them." The only thing wrong with this report is that the DAR was not founded until October 1890, and Jackson's tenure as president lasted from 1829 until 1837. Fort Knox itself was established by Congress on January 16, 1932.

Despite the obfuscation of the Fed, we do know it controls the money supply, the cost of money; that the big banks who wrote the original legislation still control it, if not by a vote majority, financial influence (follow the money); that the chairman most often has a Wall Street background or financial interest affiliated with the big banks and money elites; that the Fed is not open to public scrutiny; that some of the information on its Web site is deliberately indirect or slanted; and that it has a monopoly with the people's money.

Here's the explanation of ownership this writer received from the Federal Reserve Board's Freedom of Information Office:

"The ownership of Federal Reserve Bank stock is in the nature of an obligation incident to membership and does not carry with it the attributes of control and financial interest ordinarily attached to stock ownership of corporations that are operated for profit. The amount of stock that a member bank is required to own (three percent of its capital) is specified by law, based on its capital, **and the largest banks, therefore, hold proportionately more shares** [emphasis added]. Because each member bank only has one vote, however, the amount of stock held is of **limited significance** [emphasis added]. The stock may not be sold or pledged as security for loans, and dividends are limited by law to six percent per annum. Accordingly, dividends received by the stockholders of the Federal Reserve Banks are not related to the Reserve Banks' holdings of federal government debt."

I wonder if any of the Fed stockholders would like to swap their holdings limited to six-percent dividends? The bankers wrote the law that prohibits this and keeps the ownership among the same elites that bought the original stock. Former Federal Reserve Chairman G. William Miller once stated that any interest above three percent was attributable to inflation. Greenspan has been quoted as saying the economy cannot grow faster than 2.25 percent annually without activating inflationary pressures. If that's true, the Fed stockholders not only get the three percent profit but also are protected with a three-percent inflationary cushion. Their profit also is guaranteed with no risk, not to mention that the Fed assures the banks won't go belly up.

As for the equal vote of the twelve reserve banks, remember that the financial clout of the big banks influences the smaller banks and that all of the bank presidents are selected by bank stockholders. Most, if not all, have a common interest, their own. You won't find any farmers, school teachers, or laborers as presidents of any of these reserve banks. The officers all have bank or financial backgrounds, although the system was deliberately structured to sound democratic.

MISCONDUCT REMOVAL

Although the Fed openly discusses how officials of the Federal Reserve banks are appointed, little is ever said about how they are removed for misconduct, misfeasance, or malfeasance in office. According to Mullins (p. 31), the removal of any officer or director of any Federal Reserve bank in the original House bill was subject to approval by the president. But the Senate changed this and gave the power to the Federal Reserve Board.

Concludes Mullins, "We no longer know what the conditions for removal are, or the cause." Only one officer had been removed "for cause" at the time he inquired after thirty-six years of Fed operation, Mullins said he was told by the Assistant Secretary of the Federal Reserve Board. But the name and details of the matter were withheld as a "private concern" between the individual and the Reserve Bank concerned, and the Federal Reserve Board, he added.

So, the Fed polices itself in privacy. Its officers can't be impeached like members of the Supreme Court or cabinet and other government officials who can be removed by the president or impeached.

The Fed also is shielded from suits under the Federal Torts Claims Act, according to a ruling by the Ninth Circuit Federal Court of Appeals. The court held the Federal Reserve banks are independent, privately owned, and locally controlled corporations and not federal instrumentalities for purposes of a Federal Torts Claims Act. But the court added, "The Reserve

Banks have properly been held to be federal instrumentalities for some purposes." So, sometimes the Fed is federal and sometimes it's private. Clear?

Each Federal Reserve Bank has nine board members divided into three groups—Class A, B, and C directors. The first two classes and the bank's president are elected by the stockholders, and the Class C directors are appointed by the Board of Governors in Washington. Election of the bank's president also is subjected to approval of the board.

BUT WHO OWNS THE FED?

Trying to get a clear answer to this question is like Diogenes trying to find an honest man at high noon with a lantern. You will get various answers from historians, writers, academicians, and obfuscation from the Fed itself, but one thing you won't get is the clear, concise, understandable answer you want.

The late historian Antony Sutton, in *The Federal Reserve Conspiracy*, stated (p. 107): "The Federal Reserve is a private system owned by the banks. Fed control over money is a private monopoly granted by Congress." He said it is also noteworthy that writing on the Federal Reserve glosses over the private ownership, "yet the very aspect of the Federal Reserve that needs to be publicly discussed is its private nature, who owns what and what advantages accrue to ownership." That's the riddle wrapped in the enigma that should be cracked.

Sutton, a former economics professor himself, claimed that with few exceptions "academic economic departments are willing pawns of the modern money trust or the Federal Reserve System" and that he could speak firsthand of "the abysmal ignorance" of the UCLA Economics Department in the early 1960s.

That brings us to a couple of academic defenders of the Fed in essays written for the Internet. They are Dr. Edward Flaherty of the University of Charleston and Bill Woosley who teaches economics at the Citadel in Charleston, South Carolina.

Flaherty takes exception to authors Eustice Mullins and Gary Kah who, he said, wrote that the Federal Reserve Bank of New York controls the entire Federal System and is owned largely by foreigners. Kah, Flaherty said, asserted that foreigners use their control of the New York Fed to manipulate the U.S. monetary policy and to further their global goals, "namely the establishment of the sinister New World Order."

Relying on the structure, voting rights and appointment of officers, and the naming of the Federal Reserve Board members by the president plus the stock ownership arrangement published by the Fed, and the fact that the Fed returns large sums of money to the Treasury Department, Flaherty challenges the conclusions of Mullins and Kah. One thing he does not go into is that all the tax money collected by the IRS is deposited in Federal Reserve banks. So, who gets the use of this money until a portion of it is returned to the Treasury?

Flaherty doesn't seem to be absolutely sure about his conclusions. "It 'does not appear' that the New York Federal Reserve Bank is owned, either directly or indirectly, by foreigners," he states. But he doesn't list any stockholder names.

Flaherty also questions the sources of the two writers who list the ownership of Fed stock—Mullins as the Federal Reserve Bulletin, which Flaherty claims never included shareholder information, and Kah whose sources were unnamed Swiss and Saudi Arabian contacts. The lists of the two writers also differ.

While Flaherty's essay criticized Mullins and Kah, it offered little more than information that can be had from the Fed's Web site or the reports it sends to Congress.

Woolsey offers much the same argument as Flaherty in attacking "the conspiracy theorists" but not anyone in particular. His essay is largely a defense of the Fed, and one

gets the impression from it that the Fed is nothing more tha
an altruistic organization formed to do nothing but good for
the nation and its people and operates for nominal profit. If so,
then why all the cloak-and-dagger secrecy from Jekyll Island
that has continued to this day?

Even Griffin, who attended the College of Financial
Planning at Denver in preparation for writing his book, claims
the concept that the Fed is privately owned is a "legal fiction."
He calls it "a cartel protected by federal law."

That doesn't alter the fact that private stockholders have
owned it from the start and still do, and that it is run from
Wall Street (via money and influence) regardless of the façade
of a democratic structure. It is also obvious that (arguably
because some like Flaherty disagree) a costly middleman
would be removed if Congress abolished the Fed and returned
the issuance of money to the federal government—either to the
Treasury Department or Congress.

This would, of course, return the management of the
nation's money entirely to politicians, but they are already in
the process by endorsing the Fed's unconstitutional operations
and fawning and fuming over Alan Greenspan's appearances.
They also offer little oversight of the Fed and its reports. Ralph
Nader, as an example, contends that congressional hearings,
rather than investigating the operations of the Federal Reserve,
invariably become contests to see which member of Congress
can utter the most fulsome praise for the Fed and its current
(at the time) chairman, Alan Greenspan.

This writer can recall an account of one appearance of
Greenspan in which Senator Richard Shelby (R-Alabama)
asked him to resist all efforts of Congress to take any of the
Fed's authority away, because it was doing such a great job.
Another hard questioner was Senator Barbara Mikulski (D-
Maryland). She wanted to know if Greenspan was wearing a
new tie for his appearance at the hearing. Former Senator Phil
Graham (R-Texas) of the Senate Banking Committee went out

. his way in the spring of 1999 to tell Greenspan he would go down as a great Fed chairman. The obsequious performances of these senators are a threat to a weak stomach.

Even if the Fed operations were returned to the Treasury or Congress, a system could be worked out with checks and balances much like those in the Constitution to ride herd on those selected to operate it. There would always be threats against it by those seeking an advantage just as there is against the Constitution. But a system of accountability could be established.

One problem with any system of fiat money is that the Constitution forbids Congress from using paper money not backed by gold or silver. So a fiat money system has been operating unconstitutionally for about a century. A constitutional amendment could take care of this problem if Congress decided not to return to a gold or silver standard and to legally use a fiat money system not run by the Fed.

FED TOOLS

The tools of the Fed for controlling monetary policy include the discount rate (the charge to banks for money borrowed), open market operations (where the Fed buys and sells securities to control the money supply), and reserve requirements for member banks. The Federal Open Market Committee (FOMC), which consists of the seven reserve members in Washington, is selected by the president and approved by the Senate, plus five of the presidents of the twelve regional banks. FOMC manipulates the money supply by purchasing or selling government securities. It meets in secret but issues a brief report a few weeks after decisions are made. Transcripts of the meetings are destroyed.

The FOMC elects the chairman of the Board of Governors (Greenspan as of this writing) as its president and the president of the New York bank as its vice chairman.

With the three tools listed above, the Fed has been able to alter the federal funds rate—the rate that banks charge each other for overnight loans. Perhaps it should be noted here that Martin Mayer in *The Fed* argues that the tools the Fed once used to control the economy are no longer operable because of changing market conditions. He contends that "today's Fed has a multifaceted problem and only one tool, short-term interest rates."

As an example of the clout of the New York Federal Reserve Bank, its presidents have permanent membership in the FOMC and votes at all meetings. The representation of other presidents of the twelve regional banks is staggered. So, it's the clout and influence that counts. As an example, in the early days of the Fed, do you suppose that presidents of banks in the hinterland had as much influence in policy decisions as Paul Warburg or J.P. Morgan? These regional banks have grown, but their clout when it comes to policy is still not equal to the New York bank where most of the financial actions are still transacted.

There have never been any in-depth studies of the Federal Reserve System, although the General Accounting Office (GAO), the investigative arm of Congress, has made a couple of limited audits. They focused only on the Fed administrative operations and did not cover the broader subjects of its secret setting of interest rates, stock ownership and profit benefits of owners, the connection with foreign banks, gold transfers, and many other questions.

In the argument of who owns the Fed, it doesn't appear to be unreasonable to assume that the banker class that set it up controls it and runs it and also owns it. Follow the money.

ABOLISH THE FED

This unique and unconstitutional quasi-governmental, money-handling institution is not needed and should be done away with. It is kin to a middleman brokering the government's money. It is somewhat comparable to the relationship between brokers and Wal-Mart. Wal-Mart cut out the brokers and went directly to its suppliers to buy its goods cheaper. The government could do the same by eliminating the money middleman.

As noted, the Fed has always operated in as much secrecy as it could get away with. From the start, the bankers who planned the Fed raised money to propagandize and mislead the public about the true nature of it. They chose their men to head it and unconstitutionally took Congress out of the process with Congress' approval.

As previously noted, if the nation went back to the gold standard, the Fed would not be necessary. But there is another simple way to reduce the nation's debt and annual interest payments. And that is by the Treasury issuing its own currency instead of going through the Fed. It would still be fiat money, but the money would be the people's money, and the supply could be expanded or retired as the economy warranted it in times of economic weakness or strength.

Former Congressman Jack Metcalfe (R-Wash.) is one of several observers to wonder why the people are paying to rent the Federal Reserve's paper money when the Treasury could issue paper money the same way it does coins. Don't expect this to happen. There is too much at stake, and the banks have too much to spend to defeat any legislation that would abolish the Federal Reserve System whose name was even planned as a misleading misnomer.

The Federal Reserve System, Mullins charges "…is the product of criminal syndicalist activity of an international consortium of dynastic families comprising what he terms 'The World Order.'" Remember the words of former President Bush? The eight-trillion-dollar-plus national debt created with Federal Reserve fiat money can never be repaid, although both Democrats and Republicans talk about it from time to time as they did over the phony budget surplus at the start of the Bush II administration.

That's where the nation is—at least eight-trillion-dollar-plus in debt and probably more with no way out and headed for a New World Order without the sovereignty we all once held so dear. The state of this bondage received its major jump start in 1910 when Nelson Aldrich's private railroad car rolled southward from Hoboken, New Jersey, with a pack of banker jackals that worked out details of the plot on Jekyll Island.

CHAPTER VII

THE SYSTEM

The Fed operates under a debt-money system common to European central banks under which it was patterned. It may take an expert from one of the elite schools of finance to manipulate the nuances of it for the most obfuscation and profit, but the broad outline of how it works is comprehensible.

When the Rothschilds and other elite banking families abroad, who had control of the money and credit of European nations via central banks, decided to set up a similar system in America, the foundation they used for the bank was the debt-money system. They gained control of U.S. banking by offering money and political inducements to those in power and using front men like J.P. Morgan.

The system is explained by various writers. One book that outlines it clearly and simply is *The Truth in Money* by Theodore R. Thoren and Richard F. Warner (Truth in Money, Inc., Chagrin Falls, Ohio 4422). The authors point out that the Fed creates the money it lends, and it assumed this authority although a constitutional amendment was never passed to take the authority away from Congress, which constitutionally still holds it.

When the Fed makes a loan, it has to create a debt. It's a paper transaction, and it creates money out of nothing. The Fed also sets fractional reserve requirements for its banks. This is a common practice by banks of retaining only a fraction of their deposits to satisfy demand for withdrawals. In other words, the banks lend out your deposits several times for profit.

When the Fed makes a loan, the government goes into debt for money that should belong to the American people, not private bankers. In short, the American people go into debt to something their government created. Thoren and Warner explain that in a debt-money system, there is never enough money or credit to pay off all of the borrowed principal plus the interest, because when the Fed creates the money it lends, only the principal is created and not the interest due. Under this system, there is never enough money or credit to pay off all the borrowed principal plus interest.

Here's another explanation from the late Dr. Martin A. Larson, a Fed critic, as quoted by the *American Free Press*: "…the Fed bankers obtain government securities for nothing, collect billions of dollars of interest thereon from the taxpayers, and use them as a reserve to create credit—i.e., lend checkbook money at high interest rates equal to ten times the face value of the securities they obtain scot-free." Wonderful, isn't it?

Griffin, in *The Creature from Jekyll Island,* also elaborates on the working of the system and (p. 573) asserts, "The Federal Reserve is the world's largest and most successful scam." He claims that the Fed has failed miserably in its mission to stabilize the economy—presiding over a couple of crashes, five recessions, a stock market Black Monday in 1987, and the Great Depression. In addition, inflation has destroyed more than ninety percent of the dollar's purchasing power since 1914, and the United States has become the largest debtor nation in the world. The Fed has financed World Wars I and II and all of those in between and after.

Griffin lists seven reasons why the Fed should be abolished. First, he claims, it is incapable of achieving its stated but phony objective of stabilizing the economy; "it is a cartel operating against the public interest, and it is the supreme instrument of usury; it generates inflation which is the most unfair tax of all; it encourages war, destabilizes the economy and is an instrument of totalitarianism."

Carroll Quigley in *Tragedy and Hope* (p. 534) notes that when President Roosevelt was borrowing from the private bankers via the Fed and running up the national debt during the Depression years, he had the power to issue fiat money like Lincoln did in the form of greenbacks. Of course, the Fed uses fiat money, too, but the difference is it is public money made private on which the bankers set and collect interest. The power was never used, although FDR did use unconstitutional socialistic measures to deal with the Great Depression.

The Fed has often used the slogan that inflation is caused by "too much money chasing too few goods." The cause of inflation as well as cyclical depressions and unemployment, however, is money going for usury, not to retire debt or stimulate the economy. The inflation-causing emphasis now seems to be directed at labor, both the low unemployment rate and high wages, as well as plant capacity. U.S. workers have been losing out relative to workers elsewhere thanks to the trade agreements and the multinationals chasing low labor rates across international borders.

It is sad when Wall Street investors cheer because labor wages fall and unemployment rises. But the little guy is not supposed to share in a robust economy that can never get too robust because the Fed has a governor on it.

One of the foremost pioneers of monetary reform in England at the time of the Great Depression, Arthur Kitson, wrote *The Bankers' Conspiracy* (1933). Kitson noted that a debt-free paper currency of the people "can be easily controlled and its issues regulated to the public needs." This is a system for employing the national credit for productive purposes which belonged to the public, Kitson wrote, but the bankers persuaded (the English) Parliament to adopt a bill which set up a debt-money system based on gold at the time. Kitson called this a conspiracy on the part of certain international financiers to control the world's economy. It should be noted that Griffin doesn't think this fiat debt-money system shifted from private bankers to the government will work. He advocates a metallic standard.

The long-term economic health of the United States won't get any better until Congress takes back its constitutional authority to create money and sets up a money system either based on silver and gold or debt-free paper of the people. As mentioned, Lincoln did this during the Civil War to pay off war debts rather than borrow from New York banks at absurd interest rates. It might have worked except the banks got Congress to pass a law to strip the "Greenbacks" of their full legal tender status.

The banks finally got control of the nation's money and credit in 1913 when they connived to get the Federal Reserve Act passed in Congress. Here's how Thoren and Warner sum up that law: "A money system built on an unsound law will do exactly what our money system is in the throes of doing right now: collapse. This is why it is useless to tinker with the present system. What we need is monetary reform, not more tinkering," they contend.

LINDBERGH, ET AL

There are other good books available on the history of the Fed and how it works as well as those active historically in trying to set up the New World Order. One very good book on the political maneuvering to set up the Fed is *Lindbergh of Minnesota* (Harcourt Brace Jovanovich Jr., New York, 1973) by Bruce Larson. This biography of Charles A. Lindbergh, Sr., details the fight against the money trust by Lindbergh, the famous aviator's father. Congressman Lindbergh opposed the plan to set up the Federal Reserve System and said it would be "a private corporation" (p. 128). He also noted the banks forming the corporation would own it.

Lindberg was opposed vigorously by the *New York Times*, whose founding was backed by J.P. Morgan, a CFR member and alleged front man for the Rothschilds. Lindberg showed as much courage in fighting the bankers as his more famous son did in fighting the Atlantic Ocean. He charged "the... bill proposes to incorporate, canonize, and sanctify a private monopoly of the money and credit of the nation..." (p. 161). He quoted Abraham Lincoln toward the end of the Civil War (p. 125-26) as being as concerned about the money powers of the country as the war itself:

"...It has been, indeed, a trying hour for the Republic; but I see in the future a crisis approaching that unnerves me and causes me to tremble for the safety of my country. As a result of the war, corporations have been enthroned and an era of corruption in high places will follow, and the money power of the country will endeavor to prolong its reign by working upon the prejudices of the people until wealth is aggregated in a few hands and the Republic is destroyed. I feel at this moment more anxiety for the safety of my country than ever before, even in the midst of the war."

Mullins' work is corroborated by others such as Dr. Carroll Quigley, who weaves the story in and out of his thirteen-hundred-plus-page opus, *Tragedy and Hope,* as well as *The Anglo-American Establishment.* He confirms the existence and origin of the conspiracy. In *The Anglo-American Establishment*, Quigley laboriously details the membership, family connections, origin, and purpose of the Rhodes plan and clearly labels it a conspiracy. Gary Allen adds clarity to the story in *None Dare Call it Conspiracy* (Concord Press, PO Box, 2686 Seal Beach, CA 90740) and other works. So does James W. Wardner in *The Planned Destruction of America* and Kitson in *The Bankers' Conspiracy*, already referred to and several other works plus congressional hearings.

CHAPTER VIII

NEW WORLD ORDER

Establishment of the Federal Reserve System and other central banks controlled by the elites was just one leg of a larger plan for a world bank and world currency, according to some writers. The new bills being issued by the Treasury Department ostensibly to control counterfeiting are evidence of the new one-world currency plan, according to Gary H. Kah in *En Route to Global Occupation.* Kah, a former high-ranking government liaison, said plans were underway for a new international currency by several major countries in addition to the United States.

The International Monetary Fund and World Bank were established by liberals, Fabian Socialists, and Communists to promote the one-world concept of the elites following World War II. The plan is for one-world everything and is gradually being put into operation through the United Nations, World Trade Organization (WTO), and World Court in addition to the IMF, World Bank, and regional organizations such as NAFTA.

One note about Fabian Socialists: They differ from Communists only in approach and methods. They prefer a gradual approach through legislation rather than force and direct confrontation such as the Communists and some other groups such as the ACLU.

There are several groups promoting the one-world concept that include Fabian Socialists but are somewhat unique in their structure and membership. They include: the Council on Foreign Relations (CFR), the Trilateral Commission (TC), the Bilderbergs, the Order of Skull and Bones, the Pilgrim Society, the World Constitution, and Parliament Association (WCPA). Then there is the Illuminati, the forerunner of many of these groups, and the Masons and The Club of Rome.

The CFR is an extension of a group in London called the Round Table, itself an extension of the Rhodes Secret Society and the so-called Milner Group formed in England in the later half of the seventeenth century by influential people such as Cecil Rhodes and supported by the Rothschild banking family. The purpose of the Milner group was to promote and extend the British Empire and regain control of the United States, if possible. Rhodes scholarships are financed by the Rhodes Trust set up to recruit and influence young people in government and finance such as Bill Clinton. These Rhodes scholars hold positions in government, the press, foundations, education, and other influential professions.

The theory behind the Rhodes scholarships and The Round Tables (formed in several countries including the CFR in the United States) was to influence important people who would, in turn, influence the masses, according to Carroll Quigley in *The Anglo-American Establishment* (Books in Focus, Inc., New York, NY, p. 113). Rhodes who exploited the wealth of South Africa was behind the creation of these related organizations whose goal was to preserve the super-rich ruling class by gaining the world's wealth through control of governments and resources. These organizations overlap and interlock and some have the same members. There are some differences as is evident in their structure.

THE COUNCIL ON FOREIGN RELATIONS (CFR)

It was an offshoot of the Round Table groups, as mentioned. It represented a London-U.S. power structure designed to control both governments and was considered a foreign branch by the Royal Institute of International Affairs (RIIA). RIIA was another extension of the Milner Group. Some writers go so far as to say the London connection maintains the United States even now as a British colony. It is obvious that the CFR has become very active in planning the United States' future, especially in foreign policy and global economics.

The London connection and influence surfaced clearly in the administrations of Woodrow Wilson and Franklin Roosevelt, although there was evidence of it before that. Secrecy has been one of the CFR's tenets. Although it has been going more public recently, the minutes of its policy meetings are still secret. Quigley clearly designates the Milner Group, from which the CFR originated, as a conspiracy. He also says that group almost destroyed Western Civilization (*The Anglo-American Establishment*, p. 309).

The CFR was formed after World War I in the early 1920s, but the London connection existed well before that with the Rothschilds in firm control of J.P. Morgan and other banking and political interests. The object has been centralization of power to control not only banking but the wealth of the entire world, in other words, the so-called "New World Order." While the members are made public except when they request not to be, the minutes of the meetings are not. Its agenda is clearly against America first and the protection of U.S. sovereignty.

THE TRILATERAL COMMISSION (TC), as the name implies, includes planning by the leading ruling classes of Japan, Europe, and North America. It was formed in 1973 by David Rockefeller and Zbigniew Brzezinski, who became Jimmy Carter's security adviser. The reason it was formed was because of the rapid economic growth and power of Japan following World War II. The Trilateralists are involved in the domestic economies of the three areas mentioned and also interlock with the CFR and Bilderbergers on foreign policy.

The Trilateral Commission meets secretly but reports what it wants to be known later. Holy Sklar, who edited the book *Trilateralism* (South Bend Press, Boston), notes: "Trilateralists are not only concerned with managing international events. They are determined to manage North American, West European, and Japanese democracy, fitting these societies ever more closely to the needs of global capitalism." The public has no meaningful participation in the TC decisions. Memberships cross party lines and include the establishment elite.

BILDERBERGERS

Some writers date the Bilderbergers to 1954 and a hotel where the founders met in Holland. Others contend it goes back to the 1930s. Its members include powerful West Europeans and North Americans but no Japanese. It is involved in the global aspirations of the elite of these continents, is super-secret, and prefers no publicity whatever, not even its membership list. Peter Thompson of the London Collective, State Research, writes in *Trilateralism* (p. 158): "Bilderberg is not the only means of Western collective management of the world order; it is part of an increasingly dense system of transnational coordination." He adds:

"Democratic interference in foreign policy is avoided, in so far as possible, throughout the Western capitalist democracies." In other words, the elites don't believe that the public at large can understand momentous political decisions so they "voluntarily" plan their future for them but not with their concerns even remotely a major priority. In *The Case Against Global Economy* (p. 27), it is noted that the Bilderberg group "... played a significant role in advancing the European Union and shaping a consensus among leaders of the Atlantic nations on key issues facing Western-dominated transnational systems."

THE ORDER OF SKULL AND BONES (THE ORDER)

It is a chapter (322) of a German secret society, according to the late Antony C. Sutton who probably has made the most in-depth study of it. Its origins go back to 1833 when it was founded at Yale University by William H. Russell and Alphonso Taft, father of William Howard Taft. It was incorporated by the Russell Trust in 1856. Sutton writes about America's Secret Establishment, in an *Introduction to the Order of Skull & Bones* (Liberty House Press, Billings, Montana, 1986). Members are sworn to secrecy, and that in itself raises the question of how President Bush and his father could take an oath to support the Constitution and belong to the Order, not to mention other organizations such as the TC, CFR, and Freemasonry, to which the senior Bush belonged. Sutton writes (p. 31) that members of the Order "have created wars and revolutions, they have ransacked public treasuries, they have oppressed, they have pillaged, they have lied—even to their countrymen."

The core of the Order, he states, comprises about twenty families who are mostly descendants from the original settlers in Massachusetts in the United States, or old line Yankee families. The Order has penetrated government and other opinion and policy-making institutions to the extent that it determines the basic direction of American society, Sutton claimed. It is alleged to be tied to the Illuminati and also has an affiliation with Freemasonry. Sutton concludes from his research (p. 186) that the Order "is a clear and obvious threat to the constitutional freedom in the United States." He contends the CFR is on the fringes of conspiracy but states that the Order is a conspiracy because, among other things, its objectives "are plainly unconstitutional."

THE CLUB OF ROME

It was founded in the 1960s by leaders of several countries who met in Rome for the purpose. It has less than one hundred members, but they include highly professional and influential people. It has, according to Kah, "been charged with the task of overseeing the regionalization and unification of the entire world."

RELATED GROUPS—The Pilgrim Society, a suspect but probably harmless social club devoted to promoting the American and British establishment. Two other fringe groups are the Bohemian Club (of San Francisco) and the Atlantic Council.

THE WORLD CONSTITUTION AND PARLIAMENT ASSOCIATION (WCPA)—It was founded in 1959, and its goal is to replace the U.S. Constitution with a world constitution, according to Gary H. Kah in *En Route to Global Occupation* (Huntington House Publishers, Lafayette, Louisiana).

THE ROTHSCHILDS

The Rothschilds banking family of Europe is reported to have played the largest role in financing many governments and in setting up the Federal Reserve System here as well as the banking laws of England and other major European countries. The patriarch of the Rothschild family was Mayer Amschel Bauer, a Frankfurt, Germany, ghetto Jewish coin collector who changed his name to Rothschild. A shrewd investor and coin trader, he connived his way to become an adviser of Landgrave Frederick II of the province of Hesse, and later, his successor, Elector Wilhelm I. Rothschild. Rothschild soon learned that in banking the greatest profits lay in making loans to governments, not businesses and people.

He had five sons whom he set up in banking houses in five European cities. They were the International House of Rothschild in Frankfurt, London, Paris, Vienna, and Naples. It is the London branch and its affiliation with the Bank of England that we're most concerned with here. The London branch was started by Nathan Rothschild. Later, Baron Alfred Rothschild is said to have masterminded the details for the Federal Reserve System in the United States, although the overall scheme had been planned years in advance.

One of the largest crimes against the people has been the creation and operation of the constitutionally questionable Federal Reserve System by the same elites who are allegedly trying to establish the New World Order. They have to first establish an international currency by destroying the dollar and placing the United States hopelessly in debt. They're doing a pretty good job of it, having reduced the dollar to a worth of a just a few cents since 1914 when the Fed began operations. The United States now has a deficit tab of about eight trillion dollars.

Another big step toward this world-order goal was accomplished in the fall of 1996 when European countries agreed to create a common currency. It went into operation in January 1989. That begs the question, how long before the U.S. dollar will be integrated into a one-world currency? Any total world economic order would mean a sovereign nation like the United States could not call its own economic shots. That would be planned for us, and it would be useless to complain to our elected officials about it.

Historians may still be debating the causes of World War I. There doesn't seem to be any doubt, however, that the international bankers knew what was going to happen. Some researchers and writers even charge they conspired to bring it about. In any event, Frank A. Vanderlip, president of the National City Bank, New York's largest at the time, recalls (*From Farm Boy to Financier*, D. Appleton-Century Co., Inc., New York, 1935, p. 234) an incident that proves it. He notes that James Stillman, chairman of the bank, wired a coded message to Lord Revelstoke of Baring Brothers asking "if there will be war." A return message said, "War is inevitable." Despite Serbia's apology for the assassination of an Austrian archduke and other ongoing negotiations, Lord Revelstoke knew there would be war anyway. He was proved correct a few days later.

COLONEL EDWARD MANDEL HOUSE

A Texan was a close operative of the insiders here and abroad who were accused of being behind the schemes mentioned above. He also was instrumental in pushing, at the behest of the international planners, the League of Nations. His name was Colonel Edward Mandel House, a native Houstonian who was educated in Great Britain. House's socialistic ideas were set down in his book, *Philip Dru, Administrator* (B.W. Heubsch, New York, 1912), and were enacted into law by his friends, Woodrow Wilson and Franklin D. Roosevelt. They included the excess profits tax, unemployment insurance, a flexible currency system, and the income tax. The latter was needed to pay interest on the national debt, which was run up at full speed to pay the bankers' interest.

One way to correct some of these abuses is simply by enforcing the law. It is a violation of the Constitution to advocate the overthrow of U.S. sovereignty for a new unconstitutional order, world or otherwise. And that brings up the question of whether the Trilateral Commission constitutes a cabal? David Rockefeller, of course, says no. So did Jeff Frieden, then director of the independent Publishing Fund of the Americas writing in *Trilateralism* page seventy-three:

> The Trilateral Commission is not a cabal or conspiracy... It is the international forum for discussion and decision making of imperialist finance in an unstable age. With ties to every major imperialist government, every transnational bank and corporation, and every major imperialist think-tank, its power is significant—a concerted power based on a commonality of interests and concerns rather than a blood oath.

But Frieden goes on to say "...a major component of Trilateralism is the attempt to bribe, threaten, and cajole the people of the advanced capitalist countries into supporting the internationalization of capital." It tries to convince these countries, adds Frieden, "that international economic interdependence is better than nationalism." That sounds anti-sovereign, doesn't it?

Also writing in *Trilateralism*, William Tabb, an economics professor at Queens College, City University of New York, notes the Trilateralists have a restructuring design for the world economy. Tabb wrote that the design is being resisted on several fronts, including members of their own class. He also points out that the TC is an "...institution created by the most powerful of the world to shape our collective destiny." Remember, these powerful elites are not elected by the people.

How would you like to look up some morning and see a couple of men in your office offering to volunteer to run your operation for you, free? They would do the planning and not even charge you for their services. You won't find many charitable groups like that. But something doesn't seem to add up here, you would probably say. And you would be right. This charitable group wants something. Well, that's what happened at the State Department on September 12, 1939.

According to writers Laurence H. Shoup and William Minter, CFR members Hamilton Fish Armstrong and Walter H. Mallory offered the Council's services with the Rockefeller Foundation picking up the tab. The aim, reports Shoup and Minter in *Trilateralism*, "was to directly influence the government" (p. 137). And said Barry Goldwater, in *With No Apologies* (p. 276), "From that day forward, the Council on Foreign Relations has placed its members in policy-making positions with the federal government, not limited to the State Department."

Even Ronald Reagan stacked his administration with Trilateralists, including Secretary of State George Shultz and Defense Secretary Casper Weinberger. As Goldwater wrote, "Almost without exception the members of the CFR are united by a congeniality of birth, economic status, and educational background" (p. 278). The senator, who told it like it was, also noted that "since 1944, every American Secretary of State, with the exception of James F. Byrnes, has been a member of the CFR." (Mullins points out, however, that Byrnes was Bernard Baruch's man [p. 17].) The appointment of Madeleine Albright, Colin Powell, and Condoleezza Rice keeps the string going. The CFR has staffed almost every key position in government since FDR, according to Gary Allen in *None Dare Call It Conspiracy* (Concord Press, Seal Beach, California).

JUST CONCERNED CITIZENS

But David Rockefeller says the TC, which he founded, is just "...a group of concerned citizens interested in fostering greater understanding and cooperation among international allies." His late brother, Nelson, topped him. At his vice presidential confirmation hearings, Allen notes he called the Rockefeller control over the U.S. economy a "myth" and added,

"We have investments, but not control." It is well documented that the Rockefellers have spent millions of dollars to control U.S. foreign policy and make it fit their agenda by placing their geldings in high government offices.

David Rockefeller (*Wall Street Journal*, April 30, 1980) uses words like "extremists," "radicals," and "small-minded" to describe those who call the TC a "cabal" and question its goals and motives. But Goldwater said, "It is intended to be the vehicle for multinational consolidation of the commercial and banking interests by seizing control of the political government of the United States (p. 280)." And the senator, who was labeled a warmonger by the Trilateralists in his 1964 presidential bid, did refer to the TC as an "international cabal."

In his *Memoirs*, the old retired banker and scion of the oil-monopolist John D. Rockefeller clan wrote:

"For more than a century, ideological extremists at either end of the political spectrum (that's you and me if we disagree) have seized upon well-publicized incidents...to attack the Rockefeller family for the inordinate influence they claim we wield over American political institutions. Some even believe we are part of a secret cabal working against the best interests of the United States, characterizing my family and me as 'internationalists' and of conspiring with others around the world to build a more integrated global political and economic structure—one world, if you will. If that's the charge, I stand guilty, and I am proud of it."

Proud to be part of a secret cabal and conspiring for one world government? There you have it from Rockefeller himself.

CHAPTER IX

Here is a thumbnail sketch of the players who were at Jekyll Island and formulated the plan that ultimately was passed by Congress under dubious circumstances and became the unconstitutional Federal Reserve Act.

SENATOR NELSON ALDRICH

He has been described by some writers as the front man for the bankers and especially the Rockefellers into whose family his daughter married. His biographer, Nathaniel

Wright Stephenson, in *Nelson W. Aldrich, A Leader in American Politics* (Scribners, N.Y., 1930), writes:

"The scanty record of his youth reveals little in the way of character origins except as a matter for speculation. He was born November 6, 1841 in Foster, R. I., and traces his ancestry to Roger Williams. He led a silent, slow-maturing youth succeeded by a gradually opening manhood which at length shows a relatively luxurious nature, one that gives itself more and more in later years to the delights of art. At all stages of his development, writes Stephenson, there is an iron will, a contempt for difficulty, a belief that everything adverse can be overcome, no toleration for anyone who surrenders to his fate."

Both his parents were democrats, Anan and Abby, but he became a Republican. His business career started with work in a town store in which he later became a partner. He also became a Mason.

In his younger days, writes Stephenson, Aldrich wore a heavy black mustache and side whiskers close cut. He was seventy at the time of Jekyll Island, and his hair had receded and grown thick and white making a high forehead more prominent. His handle-bar mustache also had grown white, highlighting his brilliant dark eyes. Stephenson describes him as "a fine specimen of mature vigor." The arduous public life "had merely strengthened his will to live, to enjoy, to prevail. His powerful spirit, like the philosophers of the absolute, denied the existence of time."

In the early days of 1912, Aldrich was the subject of a sympathetic magazine article by *Munsey's*. Stephenson quotes from it. "He was a stoic; abuse rattled off him as if it were dry sand; his maxim was 'Deny nothing; explain nothing'; he had unshakable courage; he was modest, using only eight lines for his biography in the Congressional Directory; he had a contempt for self-advertising; he had a passion for accuracy; he was tirelessly industrious; his sense of organization enabled him to build up a project as if he were building a skyscraper, to stand under every stress and strain of attack."

Aldrich had met with influential bankers, including J.P. Morgan, in secret places such as his yacht, the *Omera*, and at Morgan's house in London several times before the super-secret meeting on Jekyll Island. When the meeting began, Aldrich already had been converted to an ardent supporter of a central bank similar to those in Europe such as the Bank of England. His conversion to the idea of using commercial assets as a basis for currency was, his biographer tells us, completed in Berlin. A central bank is a bank of note-issuing privilege, having the right to print and issue money, usually the people's money, as the senator intended here. When the Monetary Commission was formed in 1908 with Aldrich as chairman, he was handed an opportunity to travel abroad, to meet with the elite heads of European central banks and other dignitaries as well as to collect art and rare books.

Gary Allen (*The Rockefeller File*, p. 39) contends that Aldrich was "the insider's" mouthpiece and a front man for the positions of John D. Rockefeller. Aldrich, in addition to his work in getting a private central bank set up, also changed his position and became a staunch supporter behind income tax legislation that provided an escape hatch for the rich to avoid the tax burden by setting up foundations.

Some writers describe Aldrich as a domineering person who assumed leadership status of the group on Jekyll Island as he had the Monetary Commission for two years. He was prone to order people about and drew some confrontations because of it. In his public speeches, however, he was circumspect with an urbane tone. He was the only member of the Jekyll Island group who was not a professional banker in the technical sense, although he had long been an officer of a Providence, Rhode Island, bank and owned bank stock. That alone should have made him suspect for being in the bankers' corner on the proposed legislation. He married wealth and was a millionaire on his own by the time he left the Senate. At the Jekyll Island confabs, he resented frequent lectures by Paul Warburg, who was thoroughly versed in European central banking. Davison was reported to have prevented several clashes between them as well as others.

Aldrich wanted the administrators in the proposed regional reserve system appointed and not elected, and he also wanted Congress to have no role in their selection. Removal from congressional control, incidentally, meant the plan was unconstitutional from the start. Aldrich not only pledged all participants to secrecy even before and during the meeting but after as well, and it was two years before anything was ever printed about it. Bertie Charles Forbes, founder of *Forbes Magazine,* is credited with printing the first account of the meeting too late for it to have any impact on discussions leading to passage of legislation setting up the privately owned central bank.

Once Aldrich had been converted to the idea of a central bank, he was dead set on getting the necessary legislation through Congress. He even castigated Warburg during one meeting (not at the island) for concluding that the American people would never tolerate a central bank. "You say that we cannot have a central bank, and I say we can," Aldrich told Warburg.

PAUL MORITZ WARBURG

He was born in Hamburg, Germany, into a rich banking family that operated M.M. Warburg Company. Like the Rothschilds, the Warburgs let only family members join the business. The main stockholders in the company were the Rothschilds and the Warburg family. Warburg knew European banking "from both firsthand experience and long study...," wrote Lester V. Chandler in *Benjamin Strong Central Banker* (The Brookings Institution, Washington, DC, p. 43). Warburg, who had a thick German accent, was not an American citizen at the time he acted as the main advocate and technician in setting up a central bank, European style, for the United States. In fact, he was sent here by international bankers to do just that.

Warburg arrived in 1902 and, according to Chandler, had "...for several years before (the panic of 1907)...been an ardent advocate of banking reform." On arriving in America, he joined the banking house of Kuhn, Loeb & Company of New York as a partner. According to Vanderlip (p. 146), he came from Germany to become a partner...and to take the place of James

Loeb, who was retiring from active business. He was married to the daughter of Solomon Loeb of the international financial company where he worked. He was sent to this country for the purpose of helping to set up a central bank but not by that name.

The German immigrant had large, protruding ears, a well-cropped, wide mustache, and a bald head, except for the sides and back. The hair and mustache were black. He eschewed sideburns which many wore in that day. His forehead was large and his chin rounded. The drawing of "Daddy Warbucks" in the comic strip *Little Orphan Annie* by the late Harold Gray is a parody of Warburg and his money. It resembles him somewhat without the mustache and side and back hair.

Warburg masterminded the establishment of the Federal Reserve System, which gave control over the nation's economy to private international bankers. Without him, some observers at the time doubted that the central bank could have come into existence. Eustice Mullins, in *The Secrets of the Federal Reserve,* writes that Warburg lectured a lot at Jekyll Island and seemed to enjoy showing off his banking knowledge and used it to impress the other members. But his thick, alien accent drew some resentment even though the Americans knew Warburg had to be tolerated because of his financial brilliance.

He was the bankers' man and became the first governor of the Federal Reserve Board. Warburg's agent was Colonel Edward Mandel House of Texas, a close adviser to Woodrow Wilson and a front man for the European Rothschilds. Warburg served as governor of the Federal Reserve from 1914 to 1918, but he did not request a second term because of anti-German feelings and because of his brother, Max, who headed the German secret service in World War I. He replaced J.P. Morgan on the Federal Advisory Council. Thus, he continued to represent the Federal Reserve District of New York on the council and influence the operations of the Fed.

He was a dominant presence at the Fed meetings in the 1920s, Mullins reports, when the European central banks were planning the contraction of credit that led to the Great Depression. He was not a citizen in 1910 when he was the primary figure in setting up the Federal Reserve System, but he became naturalized in 1911 before the Federal Reserve Act became law in 1913.

He accompanied Wilson to France to negotiate peace after World War I and served as chief financial officer. His brother, Max, headed the German delegation. President Franklin Roosevelt appointed his son, James Paul Warburg, director of the budget. His son espoused financial globalism and belonged to the same groups with which his father was associated.

BENJAMIN STRONG

As were the others plotting and representing the world's moneyed elite at Jekyll Island, Strong was from a middle-class family. He was born in Fishkill-on-Hudson on December 22, 1872. His forebears were from England and migrated to Massachusetts in 1630. The family eventually settled in Northampton. Strong's father also was named Ben and had graduated from Columbia College in 1854. But his son, who was to become perhaps the most dominant force in the formative years of the Federal Reserve System in the United States, skipped college and got a job in finance at age eighteen, according to his biographer, Professor Lester V. Chandler of Princeton University (*Benjamin Strong Central Banker*, 1958, The Brookings Institution).

Strong was to become the governor of the Federal Reserve Bank of New York, which was the clout of the initial Federal Reserve System. He thought as Paul Warburg and Frank Vanderlip did that American bankers were "greenhorns" compared to European bankers, and he visited European central banks extensively and formed a close relationship with Montagu Norman, the powerful governor of the Bank of England from 1916 to 1944. He wanted the position of the Federal Reserve System to be comparable to that of the Bank of England (Chandler, p. 49). Some historians charge that Strong's close ties to Europe and especially Montagu Norman influenced the discount rate policies of the Federal Reserve which favored the Bank of England. Eustice Mullins, in *The Secrets of the Federal Reserve* (Bankers Research Institute, Staunton, VA 24401), charges that secret policies formed by the Fed and European central bankers were planned to cause the Great Depression.

Strong, who had started as a clerk in a financial management firm, moved up quickly and entered the trust company field. His big break came when he moved to Plainfield, New Jersey, where he met Henry P. Davison and developed a close relationship with him while both served as officers of the Englewood Hospital. Davison, who later became a partner in J.P. Morgan and Company, was also president of the powerful First National Bank of New York. At that time, commercial banks could not engage in the trust business, so some set up affiliations with trusts. Davison offered Strong the position of secretary of the Bankers' Trust Company, where his success led to more ladder-climbing in the Morgan empire. He also married the daughter of the president of Bankers' Trust and subsequently succeeded to the presidency. Chandler writes (p. 48), "The flat planes and deep lines of his long face, dominated by a large nose, suggested purpose, a strong will, and even a capacity for ruthlessness."

During the debate and arguments setting up the details of the Federal Reserve System, Strong had deep convictions for one central bank and not twelve, and he believed the system should be controlled from New York by bankers and not politicians, which it eventually was. According to Chandler (p. 39), he was "...unalterably opposed" to making Federal Reserve notes obligations of the U.S. government. Henry Davison, to whom he owed much for his career opportunities, and Paul Warburg spent a weekend with Strong and changed his mind on these two provisions. Strong felt the Reserve Association should be largely, if not entirely, controlled by bankers. He held many of Aldrich's views and had met with him, Vanderlip, Davison, and a few others on Aldrich's yacht and other secret places in formulating the plan from the Reserve System.

Strong's easy money policies as governor of the Federal Reserve Bank of New York encouraged the boom of the twenties which preceded the Great Depression. He was summoned to appear before a House committee in 1928 concerning gold movements and discount policies that led to the Great Depression. Strong ignored the summons and sailed for Europe ostensibly for health reasons but met with central bankers while there, according to his deputy. He died suddenly on October 16, 1928, eighteen years following the Jekyll Island meeting. He never appeared before the House.

Chandler notes that Strong was a very communicative man and left a "mass of letters, memoranda and notes" that were preserved to the benefit of his biographer. But no mention is made of the Jekyll Island meeting in Chandler's 479-page book. He does say: "After the 1907 panic Strong maintained a lively interest in currency reform, though he appears not to have participated in public discussions of the subject until 1911..." The same cannot be said of his private discussions.

HENRY POMEROY DAVISON

In every account one reads of Davison by his biographer, critics, fellow bankers, or participants in the Jekyll Island meeting, his agreeable personality and powers of persuasion come through. He was credited with settling confrontations among his colleagues and smoothing over rough encounters. He was a diplomat by all accounts. Eustice Mullins wrote that the senior partner in J.P. Morgan and Company was "generally regarded as Morgan's personal emissary and served as arbitrator at Jekyll Island." His diplomacy kept members at work at Jekyll, Mullins related.

Nathaniel Wright Stephenson, Aldrich's biographer, stated that Davison, "In managing people...had the magic touch."

In the biography of Davison by Thomas W. Lamont, *Henry P. Davison, the Record of a Useful Life* (Harper & Brothers, New York), Paul Warburg wrote of Davison: "He knew how to be silent and how to listen, how to permit the problem to unfold itself..." He also wrote Davison had a "convincing and charming personality," and that his contributions at Jekyll Island were invaluable. He added (p. 99), "Davison had an uncanny gift in sensing the proper moment for changing the topic, for giving the discussion a timely new turn, thus avoiding a clash or deadlock."

Despite his personality and diplomatic skills, Davison followed Morgan's agenda. It also was he who brought the influence of the Order of Skull and Bones into the House of Morgan. The Secret Order, which was headquartered at Yale University, listed prominent Eastern family members who have conducted U.S. foreign policy for more than a century.

Antony C. Sutton (*America's Secret Establishment, an Introduction to The Order of Skull & Bones*, Liberty House Press, 1986) tells us that after Morgan's death, the firm became Morgan, Stanley & Company. The "Stanley" was for Harold Stanley (The Order, 1908). Davison's son, H.P. Davison, Jr., was initiated into the Order in 1920. Mullins relates that Davison got eleven hundred shares of Federal Reserve Bank of New York stock and that J. P. Morgan also received a healthy share.

Unlike Strong and Vanderlip who wrote prolifically, Davison wrote little and relied more on the spoken than the written word, Lamont related. Lamont, it should be noted, also was a partner in J.P. Morgan and was brought in by Davison who also recruited Strong. So, Lamont's opinions should be considered with that background.

Davison was born in a small Pennsylvania town in a home of "modest resources." After the death of his mother when he was only nine, he lived with an uncle who, Lamont relates, had a "Puritan temperament and...limited sympathy with the exuberance of childhood." He learned the rudiments of the banking business in a small town, but "passed in amazingly few years on the widest ranges of international activity and influence," wrote Lamont. He was in his early fifties when he died an untimely death.

FRANK A. VANDERLIP

Vanderlip was born on a farm near Oswego, Illinois to parents who had migrated from Ohio. He worked on the farm until it was sold after his father's death. Then he worked in a machine shop in Aurora, which was owned by his mother's relatives.

He later got a job at the *Aurora Evening Post* as city editor and then, because he knew tachygraphy (shorthand), a friend from Aurora, Joe Johnson, who was working in Chicago at the time, landed him a job with a broker there. In this post, he read mortgages that secured bonds, and he hunted for holes in them. This was his first training in finance. His friend, Johnson, later went to the *Chicago Tribune* and secured Vanderlip a job as a reporter there. He later succeeded Johnson as financial editor of the *Tribune*.

In this post, he had contacts with Lyman J. Gage, a banker, who later took him to Washington as his secretary when Gage became secretary of the Treasury in the McKinley administration. Vanderlip later was made assistant secretary of the Treasury, a job in which he met many of the nation's leading bankers.

The Treasury job also was Vanderlip's stepping stone to the New York financial community. James Stillman, president of the National City Bank, New York, the nation's largest, became interested in Vanderlip for the way he handled the flotation of Spanish-American war bonds as assistant Treasury secretary. He hired him after Vanderlip left the Treasury in a circuitous route.

He delayed showing up at First City because the bank had bought the Custom House in Wall Street from the Treasury Department. A New York newspaper reported that this purchase, which Vanderlip claimed was perfectly legal, was a scandal. The bank saved fifty thousand dollars in taxes by maneuvering the legal time of purchase, and the Treasury left the full purchase price of 3.3 million dollars on deposit in the bank. So, to avoid scandal for the bank, Vanderlip, with letters of introduction from the bank, spent four months seeing prominent bankers of Europe (bank business).

Vanderlip, in his autobiography, *From Farm Boy to Financier* (D. Appleton-Century Co., Inc., New York, 1935, London), describes the furtive conclave at Jekyll Island in which the private bankers wrote the plan for taking over the nation's money and credit through the Federal Reserve System. He says he and the other participants felt they were doing a "public service" and didn't see the venture as a conspiracy.

He did not mention anything about denouncing, along with Aldrich after Aldrich had left the Senate, the Federal

Reserve Act, which they both helped write, to mislead the public about the purpose of the act. Eustice Mullins, in *The Secrets of the Federal Reserve* (p. 190), notes that Senator Robert L. Owing, of the Senate Banking and Currency Committee, accused Vanderlip of openly carrying on a campaign of misrepresentation about the bill.

The National City Bank of which Vanderlip was president at the time also bought a large portion of the shares of the Federal Reserve Bank of New York in 1914, according to Mullins. Vanderlip also made no reference to this in his book.

Vanderlip described himself as somewhat of a loner. In later life, he regretted that he had no interest in cards or golf like Ben Strong, Harry Davison, and other "men in the street." As he put it later, "...I am beginning to suspect that I swindled myself out of something quite precious by not playing more with my friends." But he was all business. He did not drink—another hardship at the nineteenth hole, he lamented. No one called him by his first name, Frank.

The farm boy who rose to banker dressed immaculately and was fussy about his tie at times. He wore a big brush of a black mustache on his slightly elongated face. His ears were close to his head, which was thickly covered with hair that was parted in the middle.

CHARLES D. NORTON

The son of a preacher, the Reverend Franklin B. and Harriet Dyer, Norton was born in Oshkosh, Wisconsin, and educated at Amherst University. He started his career with *Scribner's Magazine* in New York and worked with an insurance firm before becoming assistant secretary of the Treasury and then secretary to President Taft. His close association with Taft suggests that Taft could not have been uninformed about the Jekyll Island meeting. The bankers, however, thought they had a better chance of getting the central bank legislation through Congress with the Democrats and Woodrow Wilson.

Norton joined the national Bank of New York as vice president shortly after leaving his job with Taft and served at the bank from 1911 to 1918. Apparently, Norton played no major role at Jekyll Island, or at least he is not mentioned in any accounts of the meeting as having a prominent role or of being a major player as far as putting the legislation together. He apparently was there, however, to see that the banks got what they wanted out of the proposed legislation for a banker's monopoly. That Norton was an insider with the elite money power is evident from the positions he held after he left First National. They included trustee, treasurer for American Federation of Arts, Russell Sage Foundation, and Sage Foundation Homes Company in New York. He died in 1922 at the age of fifty-one.

ABRAM PIATT ANDREW (1873-1936)

Andrew was not considered one of Aldrich's closest advisers during the formation of his plan for a central bank, but he was available almost from the start to answer questions and supply aid to the senator. Aldrich had asked for an economic assistant from Harvard, and Andrew was the answer. He was from a prominent Indiana family that founded La Porte, Indiana. In addition to acting as an expert assistant for the Monetary Commission, he served as editor of publications for the group. Andrew was assistant secretary of the Treasury at the time of his appointment to assist the Monetary Commission. He later was elected to Congress, developed the famous American Field Service during World War I, and later helped found the American Legion, although he opposed the soldiers' bonus in 1932 because of the Treasury's large deficit.

EPILOGUE

The original purpose of this book was to focus on the founding of the Federal Reserve System and the machinations that went on among the bankers who planned and wrote their own legislation and bulldozed it through Congress and sold it to a gullible president and unsuspecting public.

Another reason was to keep the subject before a public that has gone along with the scheme for more than ninety years and suffered dearly in the process.

It is amazing that the founding bankers and their elite supporters in Congress were able to pull off this gigantic scam. It is even more astounding that they duped a former college professor, President Woodrow Wilson, into believing they were acting in the public interest. Wilson later lamented the fact that a few men had gotten so much control of the nation's activities.

The story would make a good cloak-and-dagger mystery, and it is surprising that it has never been made into a movie. Perhaps it is because the biographies, autobiographies, and historical accounts include no incidents of sex or other scandals outside of theft against taxpayers and the government by the straight-laced bankers.

The purpose of the book was not to chronicle the minutiae of the Fed's day-to-day operations and the arcane methods it uses to manipulate the economy. Other writers including those mentioned have done this, although none has been privy to the secrets inside the quasi-government operation and its ties to the elite class and its foreign connections.

It also was not the purpose to dwell too long on the international connection or the New World implications that other writers have mentioned. But it was necessary to go into some of this background in an attempt to make the subject more understandable to readers. I hope that effort did not detract from the story of the founding and the intrigue that went on to get the bill passed and make it palatable to the public, nor from the people who lost their lives and careers in fighting against it.

This story has always been fascinating and amazing to me because of the way the bankers were able to meet in secrecy, write their own legislation, deceive, or buy, Congress, and elect their own man, Woodrow Wilson, whom they also deceived and used, even though he was intelligent and a former college professor. How they pulled off their scam and established a banker trust at the very time the Sherman and Clayton Anti-Trust Acts were being invoked to dissolve such monopolies as the Northern Securities Company and the Standard Oil Trust is even more amazing. It has to be one of the best disguised and secretly executed swindles in history.

The system, which was conceived by bankers who wrote the law to establish it, has always been in business to protect bankers and the wealth of the elite. Despite repeated attempts to reform it and make it more democratic and responsive to the overall economic welfare, it has remained relatively unchanged since its beginning in 1913.

REFORMS

It was reformed in 1930 when more control was given to the Board of Governors in Washington, ostensibly making the twelve reserve bank presidents subordinate to the seven politically appointed Federal Reserve Board members. For practical purposes, however, this did not include the governor of the New York Federal Reserve Bank, who has always had more power than the others by influence and special privileges given to the bank, even though the New York Bank has the same one vote as the others.

As an example of the New York Bank's clout, its governor is a permanent member of the Federal Open Market Committee (FOMC), the group that makes key decisions affecting the cost and supply of money and the availability of credit. One Wall Street bigwig estimates that two-thirds of the U.S. government bond sales are in the New York federal district. In addition, a great number of the financial transactions in the country are in that district.

The reform legislation also removed the representatives of the president's—the Treasury secretary and the comptroller of the Currency—from membership in the Fed. That was supposed to give the Board more insulation from the public and from political influence. The Fed in politics? Perish the thought. Alan Greenspan jawboned Congress and the financial community on just about every subject relating to the economy and more.

The political clout of Wall Street is always involved in the selection of the Fed chairmen. Alan Greenspan and Paul Volker are examples, and they have catered to their banker constituents. The Fed's actions are proof enough of this. So, in terms of constituency, the legislative changes haven't amounted to much.

In 1978, the Humphrey-Hawkins Act called for more public disclosure from the Fed. That law ordered the agency to make public its annual target ranges for growth in the money supply (the three *M*s). The Fed chairman also was requested to appear before Congress twice a year to offer testimony. That doesn't amount to much either because of the talents of the Fed chairmen such as Volker and Greenspan who delight in obfuscation and give unintelligible answers.

THE GAME IS CHANGING

There are more important changes for Fed operations that have developed from natural forces in the changing economy. This relates to banks that once controlled the economy and were reined in or out by the Fed via interest rates and the amount of money in circulation.

Business, however, is not as dependent on bank loans as it used to be. Instead of being funded by banks, businesses are now funded directly by the sale of commercial paper to investors. Martin Mayer stated in *The Fed*, "Only one-fifth of the nation's commerce and industrial financing now comes from the banks. Bankers now take interest rates from the market instead of imposing them on borrowers...Small movements of interest rates at the banks cannot any longer generate dramatic changes in businessmen's behavior."

In other words, the traditional tools the Fed has used for controlling the economy won't work in the transition from a bank-dominated to a market-dominated world, Mayer suggests. "The challenge to the Fed is to find its place in what will be a new financial system if not a new economy," he adds.

And Alan Greenspan didn't want any constitutionally empowered outsiders like congressmen messing around with the domain of the elite technocrats working in behalf of the money class. In the late summer of 2003, he told central bankers in a speech that the U.S. economy is just too complex to reduce monetary policy to a rule-based model with inflationary parameters.

He advocated personal judgment to assess risks instead. He eschewed setting interest rates based on inflationary targets like the European Central Bank does.

"Rules, by their nature, are simple," said the Fed guru, "and when significant and shifting uncertainties exist in the economic environment, they cannot substitute for risk-management paradigms (patterns or examples), which are far better suited to policy-making."

That means the Fed technocrats can operate much better to further the interest of their clientele if they are not fettered by rules and targets. So, keep your hands off of the prerogatives of the bankers, mere legislators. The rights are theirs because they stole them more than four score and several years ago when they wrote and railroaded their central bank bill through Congress.

But the new Fed chairman, Ben Bernanke, a former Princeton professor and Fed governor, disagrees with Greenspan on setting inflationary targets. Now all he has to do is find a reliable way of gauging inflation, which some economists think has long been underestimated.

Greenspan's gastric well-being came in jeopardy whenever social security checks had to be increased because of inflation. He criticized the figures and ordered studies to back his argument, as he often did on other subjects. Maybe inflation ought to be tied to the cost of money instead of some imaginary and manipulated food basket, as some economists have suggested.

Despite his disagreement over inflationary targets, Bernanke said that he will not stray widely from Greenspan's policies. He drew little opposition either from Congress or from Wall Street, so the president is safe with his choice, and it will apparently be business pretty much as usual at the Fed.

Only one senator, Jim Bunning (R-Ky.) who has long been a critic of Greenspan's, opposed Bernanke. He was concerned the new Fed chairman would be too much in the mold of Greenspan.

A few week later Congressman Ron Paul of Texas wrote "…judging by his public statements, he [Bernanke] may be more like Greenspan than Greenspan himself." Paul quoted from a 2002 speech by the former Fed board member, in which he discussed the supposed threat of deflation at the time: "The U.S. Government has a technology, called a printing press, that allows it to produce as many dollars as it wishes at essentially no cost."

Paul pointed out, however, that there is a heavy cost; monetary inflation that decreases the value of the dollar and punishes those who save and invest.

Another Greenspan critic, Senate Minority Leader, Harry Reid, (D-Nev.) called him "one of the biggest political hacks" in Washington. The old number-cruncher did indeed relish the spotlight.

Bunning's vote came two weeks after President Bush conferred the Presidential Medal of Freedom on Greenspan who, the White House said, "has been an extraordinary leader who has make great contributions to America's economic growth and prosperity."

Some critics like Bill Fleckenstein, who manages a hedge fund in Seattle and writes a Market Rap column on his web site (FleckensteinCapital.com) disagrees with the White House's assessment of Greenspan's performance.

Fleckenstein blames Greenspan for both the stock market bubble of 2000 and the housing bubble that followed. He claims Fed minutes show the Fed was saying one thing in public, and another behind closed doors. He called Greenspan "the most incompetent and irresponsible Fed chairman in the history of the world…" and also questioned his credibility.

That may be a stretch. Whether there is merit in his criticism or not, Greenspan is departing on a high. His admirers, who almost deify him with honors, have even compared him to a rock star.

We do know that he leaves behind record budget and trade deficits, record financing from abroad, record energy prices, and probably higher inflation than reports indicated, plus a housing bubble and a lackluster job market.

Greenspan himself now admits that he contributed to the huge budget deficit by endorsing President Bush's tax cuts in 2001 when everybody thought temporary budget surpluses were forever. It is worth nothing that, at the time, Bush was considering whether to nominate Greenspan for another term as Fed chairman.

ABOVE AND BEYOND

The Fed strays beyond its original powers in several ways including jawboning Congress on taxes and other economic matters and in engaging in collusion with other central bankers. It also has, by its own legerdemain, monetized the worthless debt of some Third-World countries in an effort to protect some of the largest banks in America who had made faulty loans in the first place.

As an example of the Fed extending itself, on June 11, 2003, Greenspan appeared before a House Energy and Commerce hearing (which has nothing to do with banking) to jawbone Congress to permit more natural gas imports. What gives the Fed authority to determine what commodities should be imported or exported?

There are other economists in government as well as energy experts. But the Fed wants to be all-encompassing when it comes to the economy. It is over-extended, but nobody seems to want to clip its wings, so its chairmen get away with usurpation of authority.

In some instances, the Fed has actually acted as a central bank for Third-World countries such as Mexico, which the original Federal Reserve Act never intended. It gets away with a lot through administrative procedures, which the bankers left wide open when they wrote the original law.

It also has bailed out the Savings and Loan industry which took American taxpayers for billions of dollars as well as other banks such as Continental Illinois and Pen Square. Midwest farmers who lost their spreads because of Fed actions did not get the same treatment. But then, they were not part of the wealthy elite.

So, the central bank which is by, of, and for bankers never lets its constituency down. It rides herd on inflation to be sure the money of the elite is protected. But how much inflation should be permitted before it slams on the brakes?

Former President Clinton posed that question once. He called for a national debate on how fast the money supply can grow in relation to inflation, arguably one of the most positive things he did while president. But Robert Rubin, former secretary of the Treasury and former co-chairman of Goldman Sachs and Company, cut him off at the pass a short time later. Rubin said no such debate was necessary. Goldman Sachs, incidentally, is one of the Fed's important stockholders.

There was no debate. Why not? Because the Fed and Wall Street are more powerful than the president? As a French philosopher, Joseph Joubert, once wrote, "It is better to debate a question without settling it, than to settle a question without debating it." Try that on Rubin.

To debate the question would be an insult to the technocrats who think their profession of managing the people's money is just too esoteric for mere citizens to comprehend. But again, if that's true, what's the need for secrecy and obfuscation?

So, we don't know what amount of inflation, which stimulates middle-class activity, can be allowed. The Fed will tell us as it protects the money of the wealthy via "personal judgment." It's time to eliminate this arrogant bloodsucker and take away its money monopoly. If only we had a Congress with a backbone to do the job.

SYNOPSIS

How did a group of private bankers devise, promote and ramrod a plan through Congress to take over the money and credit of the United States at a time when anti-trust laws were being invoked to curb corporate monopolies?

Answer. With money, foreign connections, inside Congressional help, propaganda and a gullible president who believed their scheme to set up the Federal Reserve System was for the welfare of the United States.

That's what his book is about. The story begins late in the first decade of the 20th Century and involves a secret and successful scam that would make any Hollywood cloak-and-dagger mystery pale by comparison.

The perpetrators of the swindle include prominent New York bankers, a foreigner sent by European banking interests, a key senator and alleged front man for the Rockefeller interests. They pulled off a successful scheme to the take over the people's money and credit by forming the Federal Reserve System, a deliberate misnomer, since the institution formed was not Federal nor did it have the reserves its name implies.

The machinations involved tops anything Alfred Hitchcock and other Hollywood mystery producers have ever come up with. It might even rival the great Edgar Poe, the master of ratiocination himself.

The book delves into how it was done and sketches those who participated in the scheme often referred to as the greatest scam in history. It pulls together various accounts of the episode as well as biographies of some participants and quotes from one autobiography of a banker who was in on the fraud and who also was a former economics writer.

The story is astounding because the bankers were able to establish a private cartel at the very time when the Sherman and Clayton Anti-Trust Acts were being invoked to dismantle corporate monopolies such as Standard Oil.

They used as much secrecy as they could contrive to conceal their identity using first or phony names and disguising their trip from New York to an idyllic island off the southern Georgia coast as a hunting expedition. Jekyll Island, where week-long mysterious meetings took place in 1910, was then owned by J.P. Morgan and other wealthy Americans at time.

The bankers not only wrote their legislation but railroaded it through Congress in what the late historian Antony Sutton called "one of the most disgraceful unconstitutional perversions of political power in American history."

It is obvious the Fed is a failure and has not achieved its stated objective of stabilizing the economy, protecting the dollar or preventing inflation or economic cycles, some severe. As one writer points out it has presided over two stock market crashes, the Great Depression and several recessions. It has also financed several wars at least some of which its policies helped cause, some historians charge.

The dollar has declined more than 90 cents since the Fed was founded in 1913, the nation is officially about $8 trillion in debt and it may be alarmingly more, it is running record budget and trade deficits and has become a debtor nation. Some stability! Even former Fed Chairman Alan Greenspan warned of the large deficits before leaving office.

Congressman Ron Paul claims the Fed "...is inherently incompatible with real free market capitalism," and compares it to the centralized planning of prices, wages and production in the former Soviet Union.

The scheme was unconstitutional from the beginning because the Constitution forbids fiat money; Congress delegated its constitutional power to coin and regulate money to private bankers, and it also shifted some of its constitutional power to the executive branch.

The Fed's sorry record is reason enough for its abolishment, which spineless politicians will never do. At least its enigmatic and mystic nature should be stripped and its true nature should be imparted to the public via of a government-sponsored educational campaign.

The mess we are in started on a cold night in Hoboken, N. Y. in November 1910 when a private railroad car loaded with New York bankers coupled on to a train headed south. Destination: Jekyll Island.

ABOUT THE AUTHOR

Richard Sizemore is a veteran newspaperman with more than forty years' experience in writing, editing, and reporting for a wire service, daily newspapers, and trade publications. He spent more than twenty years in Washington with UPI and Fairchild Publications. He also worked for Fairchild and the *Fort Worth Star-Telegram* in Dallas and has freelanced for various publications. In Washington, his beats included the Commerce, Treasury, State, and Labor Departments and from time to time, the White House and the Federal Reserve Board, whose actions affected everyone. The story of the Fed has always been fascinating and amazing to him because it is an enigma and constitutionally suspect, but few have challenged it, and those who have tried seriously to do so have met with unkind fates. Since semi-retirement in 1990, Sizemore has devoted his time to reading, researching, and writing on this and other subjects. He writes essays on his Web site, www. sanspap.com, and he has written one other book titled *U.S. Sovereignty Under Attack.* He lives in Richardson, Texas, a suburb of Dallas, with his wife, Elizabeth.

Theodore Roosevelt: Historians still pondered why he entered the race on the "Bull Moose" ticket and helped swing the outcome to the unknown New Jersey governor from the popular President Taft. Where did Teddy get his financial backing, the bankers?

William Howard Taft: He lost votes to Woodrow Wilson in 1912 when former President Theodore Roosevelt suddenly entered the race on the "Bull Moose" ticket with plenty of financial backing.

Woodrow Wilson: Was he used by the bankers to get what they wanted? He supported the bankers' bill and even reluctantly agreed to make the reserve notes obligations of the United States "to save the bill." (Mullins,p.22). He later regretted his support and stated: "Our system of credit is concentrated in the Federal Reserve system. The growth of the nation, therefore, and all our activities are in the hands of a few men." (American Free Press)

Thomas Jefferson: He maintained that no where in the Constitution "...was Congress given the authority to establish a national bank—not even under the seemingly open-ended 'necessary and proper clause,'" according to James F. Simon (p.30) in What Kind of Nation.

President Andrew Jackson

Jackson told the bankers trying to persuade him to renew the charter of the Second Central Bank, "You are a den of vipers. I intend to rout you out, and by the Eternal God I will rout you out."

Clubhouse at Jekyll Island, where the bankers met to devise their plan for legislation to setup the Federal Reserve Board.

Abraham Lincoln: "As a result of the (Civil) War, corporations have been enthroned and an era of corruption in high places will follow, and the money power of the country will endeavor to prolong its reign by working upon the prejudices of the people until wealth is aggregated in a few hands and the Republic is destroyed."

J.P. Morgan

THE Hunt Club –

Members represented 1/6 of
the World's wealth.

CPSIA information can be obtained at www.ICGtesting.com
Printed in the USA
LVOW11s2119200315

431468LV00001B/8/P

9 781425 912444